THE ENLIGHTENMENT IN FRANCE

THE
ENLIGHTENMENT
in France

FREDERICK B. ARTZ

Oberlin College

THE KENT STATE UNIVERSITY PRESS

Frontispiece
Voltaire by Lücke
Allen Art Museum, Oberlin, Ohio

SBN 87338-032-0
Library of Congress Card Catalog number 68-21503
Copyright © 1968 by Frederick B. Artz
First Edition Third Printing
Manufactured in the United States of America
Designed by Merald E. Wrolstad

CONTENTS

PREFACE

This is an introduction to the principal writers of the Enlightenment in Eighteenth Century France. French thinkers of this century made a long series of devastating attacks on old ideas, usages, and institutions that had been handed down from the past. And, at the same time, these thinkers proposed a series of thorough-going reforms in social, economic, political, religious, and educational ideas and institutions.

France was the center of the Enlightenment of the Eighteenth Century, but there were important thinkers that belong to the movement in other countries, such as Vico and Beccaria in Italy, Lessing, Herder, and Kant in Germany, and Hume, Adam Smith, and Bentham in Britain. France, though, took the lead, and, outside of France, there were no thinkers of quite the influence of the French writers, Voltaire and Rousseau.

The whole climate of opinion was changed in France and the rest of Western Europe by these publicists and propagandists, or as they were commonly called, the Philosophes. The Eighteenth Century in France began with certain currents of opinion in the ascendancy, namely, divine right and absolute monarchy, uniformity of religious opinion (Gallicanism in France), a controlled economy (Mercantilism), and Classicism in art and literature. And the Eighteenth Century ended with a widespread belief in some form of representative and Liberal government, with the idea that religion is an individual matter, with Laissez-faire economics, and with growing Romanticism in the arts. This change of opinion was largely due to the Philosophes.

The writers of the Nineteenth Century regarded the French Philosophes of the Eighteenth Century as naive and superficial. But the anti-intellectual movements of the Twentieth Century and its totalitarian regimes make the Philosophes' emphasis on reason, common sense, and humanitarianism seem refreshing. Many of the ideas of the Philosophes had been stated or suggested by earlier thinkers, especially by those of the Seventeenth Century, but the Philosophes in giving these ideas an order and a more practical application can be considered the founders or extenders of the modern social sciences: political science, economics, sociology, ethnology, anthropology, history, and psychology.

Beneath the surface of the Eighteenth Century, there was, in France, political discontent on the part of the professional classes. Social discontent also arose as the middle classes contemplated the magnitude of the burdens imposed by the state and the inequities of the privileges enjoyed by the nobility and the clergy, and intellectual discontent grew against the tyranny of an absolute monarchy claiming to rule by divine right and the oppression of a decadent and obscurantist Church. Against this background, the Philosophes preached reform rather than revolution. Nevertheless, some of the Philosophes foresaw revolution. In 1762 Rousseau wrote in *Emile*, "we are approaching a state of crisis and a century of revolution," and in 1764 Voltaire said, "everything I see sows the seeds of revolution which will not fail to come." The Philosophes preached the pursuit of happiness and virtue. The Greeks had preferred wisdom to happiness, the Romans power, and the Middle Ages holiness.

Napoleon once said that "cannon destroyed the feudal order but ink destroyed the old monarchy." That is too simple an explanation. The French Revolution was actually the result of both: abuses of all kinds in the political, economic, and social order of the Old Regime and propaganda for all types of change. In spite of the excesses of the French Revolution and the Conservative reaction that followed it, the Philosophes' ideas of Liberalism and democracy went on to mold much of the thinking and institutions of the Western World.

I have throughout put all book titles in English, and I have consistently used "Philosophe" as an English word for the Eighteenth Century publicists and propagandists. Many of the quotations have been shortened, and to make for easier reading I have deliberately omitted the use of three dots. I am indebted to a number of colleagues for help: Robert J. Soucy, Donald M. Love, Robert E. Neil, Vinio Rossi, Peter Gay, Arthur M. Wilson, and Crane Brinton.

FREDERICK B. ARTZ

Oberlin, Ohio
January 1, 1968

1

THE PRECURSORS
OF THE PHILOSOPHES

1. The More Remote Precursors

The writers of every age, if they pay any attention to the past,
are given to choosing from earlier authors those whose views
are sympathetic with their own. So we see the Philosophes
ranging over the past, and praising writers who in some degree had ideas similar to their own, and borrowing freely from
these authors.

Most of the thinkers of the Eighteenth Century were early
trained in the Greek and Latin classics which were still the
basis of education, and the classics, either in the original languages or in translation, with their generally worldly attitudes
were used as examples of more reasonable ways of thinking
than those set up by Christianity. The common attitude of
Eighteenth Century intellectuals toward antiquity was one of
admiration, but they usually opposed a mere antiquarianism,
and held that modern man should imitate only what was
worth imitating.

An important background for the Philosophes, as for Karl
Marx later, was furnished by the ethics and some of the general attitudes of Christianity. One could never imagine the En-

lightenment appearing in Asia or Africa. The Christianity against which the Philosophes revolted was ever present in their minds, and some critics have regarded the Philosophes as "Christians in secular dress." And despite their criticism of Scholasticism, they owed something to Scholastics like Aquinas who had emphasized the value of reason inside Christian theology.

The knowledge of ancient civilization possessed by the Eighteenth Century was often incomplete and inadequate. Archeology, philology, anthropology, economics, sociology, and psychology were only in their beginnings. Pre-history and ancient civilizations before Greece were very imperfectly known. Most of the Philosophes had received a more thorough training in Latin than in Greek, and though Rousseau admired Plato, especially *the Republic*, the most quoted of ancient writers were Cicero and Lucretius. Cicero (d. 43 B.C.) was admired for his down-to-earth ethics as set forth in the *Concerning Duties*, his critical attitude toward traditional Roman religion, his belief in the essential equality of all men, his exaltation of law, and his faith in human brotherhood. Lucretius (d. 50 B.C.) was praised for his materialism,—his belief that all man could know is matter, and that all matter is made up of atoms and a void,—and some admired Lucretius for his atheism. Many other classical writers were quoted to prove one point or another.

The Eighteenth Century knowledge of the Middle Ages was woefully inadequate. Liberal Philosophes did know about the critical attitudes of Abelard, Roger Bacon, and the Emperor Frederick II. But they did not know about the worldly ideas of the Goliardic Latin poets and of the vernacular lyrics and chivalric romances of the troubadours, trouvères, and minnesingers. Accurate knowledge of what the Middle Ages were really like did not come till after 1800.

The Philosophes admired the worldliness of the Humanists of the Renaissance—especially of the Italian Humanists. They praised the Humanists' use of the classics, their detachment from myth, their praise of a life of action, their tendency to prefer ethics to metaphysics, their general worldliness, and their hard-headed eclecticism. And the Humanists prepared men to read Christian documents with skeptical detachment. From the early Protestant polemicists, the Philosophes borrowed the arguments of Luther and Calvin in their attacks on the papacy and many of the practices of Roman Catholicism. For the later Luther, after he came narrowly to define his new faith, and for much of Calvin's theology the Philosophes showed nothing but raillery and disgust.

Among the vernacular writers of the Renaissance, the Philosophes praised Rabelais (d. 1553) for his robust and wholehearted acceptance of the joy of life, and his revolt against the asceticism, Scholasticism, and superstition of the Middle Ages. But the most admired vernacular writers of the Renaissance were Machiavelli and Montaigne. The Philosophes admired Machiavelli (d. 1527) because he was the first modern writer to consider politics apart from Scholasticism and apart from any other metaphysical system. As Francis Bacon said, "We are beholden to Machiavel who openly and unmasked declared what men do in fact and not what they ought to do." It was Machiavelli's *Prince* that was especially admired, though Rousseau and Diderot preferred the *Discourses on Livy* with their defense of republicanism. Some found in the *Prince* what seemed a scientific description of political facts where, without considering theology or moral philosophy, the author described what made governments strong and weak.

Montaigne (d. 1592), though he remained a Catholic for political reasons, was a perfect skeptic, who during the religious wars in France, was contemptuous of both Catholics and Protestants. Montaigne's skepticism came partly from disgust at the quarrels of Catholics and Protestants and their mutual brutalities, partly from admiration for experimental science which was discovering a great new source of truth independent of revelation, and finally from the tales of travellers who found religions and cultures older than that of the Christians and more to be admired. His thought led to a tolerant skepticism wherein Montaigne was sure of nothing, though his thought was in nowise constructive. The Philosophes cherished Montaigne's informality, his openminded rationalism, his profound skepticism, and his great contempt for all kinds of fanaticism. Some of Montaigne's popularity among the Philosophes came also from his charming and quite unpretentious style of writing.

2. Some Foreign Seventeenth Century Precursors

Among the most important precursors of the Philosophes

were the great scientists from Copernicus through Galileo to Newton though most of their influence came through philosophers and publicists who funnelled their ideas down to the Philosophes. Most important as a scientific popularizer among the pure scientists was Galileo (d. 1642) who outlined in a popular style the aims of science, emphasizing the value of mathematics and the goal of quantitative formulation of all experience.

The greatest popularizer of scientific ideas in the early Seventeenth Century was Francis Bacon (d. 1626). Bacon was the first philosophic writer of early modern Europe to use the inductive method of thinking in his writings. The method had been used by the scientists of the Sixteenth Century, but Bacon was the first who would found all philosophic labor of the mind on a wholly new basis. If we would ascertain the hidden nature of things, we must not look for it in books, or in preconceived notions and *a priori* speculations. Above all, thinkers must give up imitating the ancients who with the exception of Democritus and a few others had observed but little and that superficially. Existing knowledge is full of prejudices, superstitions, and old wives' tales. The only hope of thinkers is to break entirely with Greek and Scholastic thought, to give up the search for final causes, and to accept the inductive method of reasoning.

Bacon was especially severe on Scholasticism of which he wrote, "This degenerate learning did briefly reign among the Schoolmen, who having strong and sharp wits and abundance of leisure and small variety of reading, but their wits being shut up in the cells of a few authors (chiefly Aristotle their dictator) as their persons were shut up in the cells of monasteries and colleges, and knowing little history, either of nature or time, did out of no great quantity of matter and infinite agitation of wit spun out to us those laborious webs of learning which are extant in their books. For the wit and mind of man, if it works upon matter worketh according to the stuff, but if it work upon itself, as the spider worketh his web, then it brings forth cobwebs of learning admirable for the fineness of thread but of no substance or profit."

Bacon did not discover the scientific method but he made the most lucid and eloquent appeal which had been made so far for its use. The end of the sciences is their practical usefulness to extend the rule of man over nature and to increase man's comfort and happiness. Bacon himself was a popularizer, not a scientist. He refused to accept the Copernican hypothesis, nor did he know some of the important scientific work of his time. He was ignorant, for example, of the scientific writings of Kepler, Tycho Brahe, and Harvey. He was no mathematician, and for all his prophetic insight, was blind to the potentiality of mathematics in the science of the future. In all these matters he stands in contrast to his younger French contemporary, Descartes. Bacon's life with its slow rise to political power and to the position of Lord Chancellor of England, and its sudden fall, when he was impeached by Parliament for taking bribes and banished from London, undoubtedly helped to attract attention to his thought. D'Alembert later dedicated the *Encyclopedia* "to the spirit of Lord Bacon," and called Bacon "the greatest, most universal, and the most eloquent of philosophers." The Convention, during the French Revolution, published the works of Bacon at state expense.

Hobbes (d. 1679) was not well known in France. But some knew about his implied atheism and his belief that nature is a machine, that nothing counts but matter and motion, and that the whole of mental life is built upon the foundation of the senses. Hobbes also proclaimed the idea that we could solve our social and moral problems if we only made our social sciences as scientific as mathematics and physics. Hobbes' doctrine that man is by nature unsocial and the enemy of his fellows, and his fearful description of primitive society found no acceptance in France though the Philosophes did have a keen sense of man's self-esteem which needs curbing and should be tied to the general interest. Nor did Hobbes' doctrine of absolute sovereignty, which embodied a conception of absolutism more far-reaching than that ascribed by medieval churchmen to the Church, find any French followers.

While Spinoza (d. 1677) was well known in France, especially to Liberal and Radical thinkers, and though the Philosophes showed little interest in his pantheism or his metaphysics, certain of his ideas filtered through. One was his belief in a rational reading of the Bible. If interpreted literally, the Bible is full of errors and contradictions and impossibilities. Spinoza denied outright the personal God of the Jews and Christians. He also pleaded strongly for toleration and religious freedom as practiced in Holland. Spinoza was the originator of the idea of the historicity of the Bible and the first to develop it with precision and clarity. The nature of things is not to be understood through the Bible, but the Bible is to be understood by the nature of things. Another idea of Spinoza's was his preference for the great materialists, Democritus, Epicurus, and Lucretius, and his admiration for Descartes' idea of one substance underlying all forms of matter. It was known too that Spinoza admired Descartes' attempt to explain all the world except God and the soul by mechanical and mathematical laws. Spinoza was likewise regarded as something of a martyr for the freedom of thought as he had been put out of his synagogue in Holland for his beliefs. Also his belief in democratic institutions was known in Eighteenth Century France. In this, including his belief in two social contracts, one to form society and another to form the state, was known to Montesquieu and Rousseau. His belief that democracy was the most reasonable form of government, that every man should be given as much liberty as possible, and that liberty should be limited only by such laws as work for the general welfare, made him one of the early prophets of democracy. Some held Spinoza's name in abhorrence. It was finally Lessing, Herder, Schleiermacher, Goethe, and Novalis who restored him to repute. Novalis called him "the God-intoxicated man." Some Eighteenth Century writers, especially those favorable to the Church, linked Spinoza with Hobbes, and regarded both as atheists, materialists, and enemies of morality.

Leibniz (d. 1716) was well known in France, partly because some of his writings were written in French. Fontenelle praised him in the Academy of Sciences as a universal genius whose mind ranged over a wide series of fields. Leibniz admired Descartes' method of systematic doubt, but condemned Descartes' tendency to ignore sense experience and the whole Cartesian conception of material substance. Leibniz' God is not like an Oriental despot, but is a sovereign bound by laws which he cannot unmake. God is a kind of constitutional king of the universe. Leibniz was thus something of a deist.

Frenchmen of the Eighteenth Century were interested in Leibniz as a great compromiser who sought to reconcile religion and philosophy, Catholicism with Protestantism, and the principles of Christianity with those of rationalism. Leibniz believed in basic human freedoms, above all in the freedom of each individual to achieve his intellectual and moral improvement. He thus was creating the ground for the "inalienable rights of man." So Leibniz is regarded by some critics as the "true originator and founder of the philosophy of the Enlightenment." Actually, Leibniz left two philosophies: one was optimistic and rather shallow, such as would win him popularity and the approbation of princes, and the other, embodied in writings published after his death, which was more profound, coherent, and logical and which resembled the philosophy of Spinoza. It was the earlier Leibniz whose optimistic philosophy was caricatured by Voltaire in *Candide*. All in all, Leibniz' influence in Eighteenth Century France was considerable.

The ideas of no two foreign thinkers of the Seventeenth Century were so well known in Eighteenth Century France as the theories of two Englishmen, Locke and Newton. Locke

(d. 1704) was the son of a Puritan, was trained in medicine, and became the secretary of Lord Shaftesbury, founder of the Whig party. Because of his Liberal views, he was forced to live in exile in Holland and on the Continent during the reactionary reign of James II. Locke early acquired a dislike of dogmatism and pedantry, and he always wrote very clearly. He was especially admired for not building vast constructions on abstract principles.

Fundamental to Locke's general position was his famous *Essay on Human Understanding* published in 1690. Here, he maintained that children entered the world with no innate ideas. At birth the mind is a blank sheet on which experience and reflection, derived from the senses, write their effects. The idea implied the natural equality of all men, and made man the result of his environment. It was just a step to the theory that if you change the environment you will breed another sort of man. From Locke's views the conclusion could be drawn that the evil we find in man is not natural to him, but is the result of bad experience, bad education, vicious institutions, and old prejudices handed down for generations. Here, as in his other writings, Locke showed himself a conscientious and close observer of facts. So it was said of him that he "raised common sense to the point at which it becomes luminous."

In his *Letter on Toleration* of 1689, Locke advocated the toleration of all religious sects except Roman Catholics and atheists. The former were excluded because they maintained a foreign allegiance to the Pope, and the latter because they lacked moral responsibility, and were not bound by oaths. Those who persecute in the name of religion violate the primal Christian commandment of love. Locke believed that religion is a matter of conscience and cannot be forced. Locke, like Newton, remained faithful to the Church of England, and in his *Reasonableness of Christianity* defended Christianity against its critics.

In his two *Treatises on Government* of 1690, Locke defended Liberal political ideas. He believed that men entered a contract to set up government to secure personal and property rights. This implies mutual obligations of ruler and ruled. Man gets a right to property by incorporating his labor in some particular object. Like his other works, these treatises on government were written for the common reader. Santayana once said of Locke's writings that "had Locke's mind been more profound it might have been less influential." The first *Treatise on Government* was a reasoned attack on the idea of the divine right of kings, and the second was a defense of Liberal political ideas and of the two revolutions that had taken place in Seventeenth Century England. Life, liberty, and property are the natural and inalienable rights of every individual. Society and government exist to protect individual rights, including the right to hold property.

Locke, in contrast to Hobbes, believed that the original state of nature was one of "peace, good will, mutual assistance, and preservation," and he also held that every man had natural rights prior to society and the state. Government had been created by men for their own security both from within and without the community, but political authority always rests on the consent of the people. Thus, sovereignty is in the people. If at any time the ruler is untrue to his trust, authority reverts to the people, and revolution is justified. The government must enforce by penalties the prescriptions embodied in the laws. The legislative is the supreme power in the government. And to protect men's liberties the powers of the government, executive, legislative and judicial should be separated.

Locke also wrote a treatise *Concerning Education* (1693) which was widely read. The aim of education is to inculcate virtuous habits, practical wisdom, good breeding, and a body of knowledge. He includes athletics and practice in a practical trade. Corporal punishment and bribery as rewards are to be used sparingly; praise and blame should be the chief stimuli to good behavior. Play should be allowed without restraint. Manners are very important, and are best taught by good example at home. Throughout Locke advocates an appeal to the pupils' interests rather than the fear of punishment as the chief motive for learning.

In Locke, Liberal political ideas first became associated closely with the scientific movement. He approached social and political questions from the point of view of a Seventeenth Century physicist and treated them exactly as if he were laying plans to dam rivers or to build bridges. All in all, Locke covered many fields—politics, religion, psychology, and education—and everywhere his emphasis was on the Liberal side of things. His works were early translated into a number of Continental languages, and his influence was immense.

Newton (d. 1727) was likewise a towering figure in both Seventeenth and Eighteenth Century thought. He made many of his scientific discoveries before he was thirty, and his great Latin treatise, *Principles*, the most important single book in the history of science, was published when he was in middle life. Newton's writings were too abstract, and required too much previous knowledge of astronomy, mathematics, and physics for the average readers — so his ideas were passed on by middlemen. Before 1789, forty books about Newton's main ideas appeared in English, seventeen in French, three in German, eleven in Latin, one in Portuguese, and one in Italian. Many of these ran through a series of editions.

What Newton stood for was what Galileo, Descartes, and other earlier thinkers had arrived at; i.e., a completely mechanical interpretation of the universe and nature in exact mathematical terms. Newton's work was a great synthesis of much of the science of the Sixteenth and Seventeenth Centuries. It was a magnificent relevation of the power of the scientific method, and placed the keystone in the centuries of discoveries in astronomy, mathematics, and physics. In Newton's writings the map of the universe was redrawn. The universe was now one huge related and universal machine. Newton's writings showed facts carefully observed and then brilliantly interrelated and interpreted. Newton humbly accepted facts and showed a deep-seated abhorrence of any theory that could not stand the test of facts. Newton remained faithful to the Church of England and accepted Jesus as a divinely inspired mediator between God and man. Being a cautious scientist, he did not try to draw materialistic deductions from his work. He did, however, believe that principles of human conduct might be discovered by scientific research, and might be embodied in a few incontrovertible laws. The later materialism of Diderot, La Mettrie, Helvétius, and Holbach derived in part from Newton. Turgot wrote in the *Encyclopedia* that Newton had at last described the land which Descartes had discovered.

The work of Newton encouraged the hope that all branches of knowledge could be reduced to a few, simple, and uniform laws which any reasonable man could understand. Reason would then enable an enlightened world to make all institutions conform to natural laws. Nature was through and through orderly and rational; hence, what was natural was inevitably identified with what was rational. The great object of human endeavor, the disciples of Newton believed, was to discover what in every field was natural and reasonable and to brush aside the accretions of irrational tradition, so that reason and the explanation of nature might more easily follow an harmonious order. The universe had always been such an order and had been created so by the hand of God. There was no idea of change or evolution or development as the Nineteenth Century came later to believe. Newton led thinkers to prize scientific methods of experimentation, observation, and generalization. Voltaire said Newton taught men "to examine, weigh, and calculate, but never to conjecture." Newton's followers believed only patient and skeptical inquiry could produce reliable results. They rejected metaphysical systems as they rejected stories of miracles. But they oversimplified problems of theology, history, ethics, politics, and other fields where the methods of scientific inquiry of physics and mathematics were not easily applicable.

Also from England came a new current of religious thought in the form of deism. This was a belief in the existence and power of God but a rejection of revelation and of the miracles and prophecies of the Bible. Deistic ideas had their roots in the thought of the Sixteenth Century, but it was pushed rapidly ahead by English thinkers of the later Seventeenth and early Eighteenth Centuries. The toleration and the free press in England gave the deists the opportunity to publish. In general, the English deists, and later the Continental deists who derived from them, believed in one supreme God who is to be worshipped by the practice of active virtues, and the repentance of men for their sins. They also believed that there were for men rewards and punishments both here and hereafter. The deists believed the essence of religion lay in morality. Deism was never a sect but represented a set of general ideas. It remained a concern of the intellectual classes, and scarcely touched the masses. Deism also stimulated a critical study of the Bible, of church history, and of all religious ideas. For some thinkers, as Diderot, deism was a halfway position between Christian religious faith and atheism. Deism in France owed more to Voltaire than to any other writer. Deism expressed the growing confidence of men in the power of reasoning and the increasing belief that the universe was a vast machine. It was the first serious attempt to adopt old religious traditions to the attitudes of the modern world.

3. Some French Seventeenth Century Precursors

First among the Seventeenth Century precursors of the Philosophes was Descartes (d. 1650). Son of a well-to-do family, he, like Voltaire later, was educated by the Jesuits. Descartes then served a while in the armies of several countries, and finally went to stay in Holland where he lived on his income, and devoted himself to his favorite subjects of philosophy and mathematics. He had become disgusted with all that he had been taught except mathematics. It is vain to look for truth in books. Rejecting all beliefs except the belief in God, he went back to a complete skepticism. All he finally believed was that he himself existed. "I think, therefore I am," he wrote. This became the foundation of his philosophy.

Descartes decided that the order of nature is invariable, and rejecting Scholasticism and all previous philosophies, he attempted to build a new philosophy. "Above all," he wrote, "I was delighted with mathematics" (which Bacon had ignored) "because of the certainty and evidence of their demonstration. I was surprised that upon foundations so solid and stable no loftier structure had been raised." Descartes went on to assert, "It is possible to attain knowledge which is useful in life, and instead of the speculative philosophy which is taught in the schools we may find a practical philosophy by means of which, knowing the force and action of fire, water, air, the stars, the heavens, and all other bodies that environ us we can employ them in all those uses to which we are adopted, and thus render ourselves the masters and possessors of nature." He believed that science would "make men the masters of everything." Descartes rejected the whole of ancient and medieval metaphysics. The structure of nature is all a matter of chemistry and physics. All animals are mere automata, and even the body of man is a purely physical machine. The structure of nature is quantitative rather than qualitative as with Aristotle and the Scholastics. These ideas circulated in his three best-known works: *The Discourse on Method* (the first great philosophic work to be written in the vernacular), and in *Meditations on the First Philosophy*, and finally, in his *Principles of Philosophy*. His principal scientific work was done in analytical geometry, optics, and general physics. So Descartes helped to fix in men's minds the mechanical pattern of the invariable laws of nature and the supremacy of reason. These laws of nature could be discovered by careful experiment and by the use of reason which Descartes exalted. He insisted that all motion can be measured mathematically. He labored on an elaboration of what he called "a universal mathematical science," a vast system which should begin like geometry with incontestable maxims and deduce from them a comprehensive philosophy of man and the world, but he died before he had accomplished much on this vast project.

The legacy of Descartes was to lay down the ideas of mechanism and mathematical analysis and reason as the guide posts of scientific thought. These general ideas rather than his elaborate metaphysics, which the Philosophes mostly ignored, were very influential in the thought of the Seventeenth and Eighteenth Centuries. Descartes' philosophy was a great force undermining orthodoxy and fostering the spirit of free inquiry, and he helped to further the idea that science could be applied to ethics, political theory, law, and the social sciences in general.

Coming down into the long reign of Louis XIV we find a number of critics who were, in some degree, forerunners of the Physiocrats, such as Boisguillebert and Vauban, the famous military engineer. Boisguillebert (d. 1714) was a severe critic of Mercantilist ideas and the whole economic situation under Louis XIV. His writings vividly portray the economic misery of the masses and the abuses of the system of taxation. He believed in a system that would allow a free flow of goods with little government interference. Money, he held, is only a means of exchange. A country may be prosperous without much money and the country which has only money and not a flourishing economic life may be wretched. He was, though, particularly concerned about giving protection from foreign competition to the French farmer. Boisguillebert proposed a series of practical reforms in the systems of tariffs and taxation, but they were never tried.

Vauban (d. 1707) condemned the whole system of taxation in France. He pointed out that a tenth of the population was reduced to beggary, half of it was on the borderline of starvation, and only about one-tenth could be accounted comfortable. Vauban proposed a single tax on all property to be paid by all classes including the nobility. The economic miseries of the peasantry in France—who formed the overwhelming majority of the population—and the anomalies, injustices, and stupidities of the regime of Louis XIV are also represented in the sketches of various types of the age of Louis XIV in the *Characters* of La Bruyère (d. 1696). So beneath the apparently smooth surface of Louis XIV's despotism, severe criticism of his regime arose.

A minor precursor of the Philosophes in the reign of Louis XIV was Saint Evrémond (d. 1703). He had been educated by the Jesuits, had served as an officer in the Thirty Years' War, then having fallen into disgrace with the French government, he had gone to live in exile first in Holland, then in England. Here Charles II granted him a pension. Saint Evrémond was a devoted disciple of Montaigne, and his writings are full of cynicism and skepticism. He was interested in ethics, politics, and literature; his outlook was cosmopolitan, and epicurean; his stock in trade consisted of doubts and denials; and he was critical of many of the aspects of the regime of Louis XIV.

That the intellectual situation under Louis XIV was changing is shown by the quarrel between the "Ancients" and the "Moderns." The quarrel had got well under way when, in 1687 Charles Perrault read before the French Academy a poem on the *Century of Louis XIV* which declared the "Moderns" superior to the "Ancients" in all things but especially in science. Boileau championed the "Ancients." It was all primarily a literary quarrel. The "Ancients" held that the literary and philosophic works of the Greeks had never been surpassed. The "Moderns" insisted that modern literary works were the equal of those of the Greeks, and that, in addition, philosophy, science, and invention had moved ahead of the

Greek achievements in these fields. This quarrel was repeated in other countries in the Seventeenth and Eighteenth Centuries; it was particularly hot in England. Backing the "Moderns" Dryden well summed up their ideas, "Is it not evident in these last hundred years, when the study of philosophy has been the business of all the virtuosi, that more errors have been detected, more useful experiments have been made, more noble secrets in optics, medicine, and astronomy discovered than in all those credulous ages from Aristotle to us?" This quarrel foreshadowed the denunciation of their predecessors by the Philosophes of the Eighteenth Century. It also contributed to a growing belief in progress; i.e., what was to be called "the gospel of perfectibility."

Fénelon (d. 1715) belonged to an ancient noble family which had distinguished itself in war, diplomacy, the Church, and literature. He was also an archbishop of the Church. Saint Simon, who knew him slightly described his appearance in his *Memoirs*, "This prelate was a tall man, well-made with eyes from which the fire and intellect gushed like a torrent, and a countenance the like of which I have never seen. He had gravity and gallantry, and what was manifest above all was elegance, refinement, intellect, grace, decorum, and nobleness. It required an effort to cease looking at him." Yet behind this elegant and distinguished surface there was a spirit of criticism of the whole order of things as they existed under the absolute monarchy of Louis XIV. He early learned Greek, and he always loved Greek literature especially Homer and Plato. After he became a priest, his first assignment was that of head of a school for girls lately converted to Catholicism. The result of this experience was his *Treatise on the Education of Girls*. Here he believed in following the nature of the pupil, in mingling work with play, and adopting instruction to the mind of the individual child. Rousseau borrowed from the book for his *Emile*. In religion, Fénelon did not believe in toleration but hated the use of force; he wanted to use only persuasion on the Protestants.

In 1689 Fénelon was appointed tutor to the grandson and heir of Louis XIV. As a tutor, he transformed a spoiled and head-strong boy into a reasonable youth. For him, Fénelon wrote his most famous work *Telemachus*. It tells the story of the wandering of Ulysses' son in search of his father. The young man is accompanied by a wise old friend who points out the excellencies and errors of the government of the countries through which they passed. These travels resemble the grand tour then fashionable among the sons of the rich and noble. In some of the states visited the people were well-ruled, and even enjoyed a sort of communism, and the way of life was simple. The people had much freedom in commercial relations, and war and aggression were unknown. The implied remedy throughout was for France to revive its old constitution, to persuade the king to respect the fundamental laws, to equalize the taxes, and to listen to the Estates General which should meet every three years. The work is full of attacks on many of the features of the rule of Louis XIV, and was the most severe criticism of that rule that had been made. The book contains the idea of the noble savage which Fénelon had got from reading the popular travel books of explorers and missionaries. Implied is the natural goodness of man. Fénelon also wrote a long and detailed letter to Louis XIV enumerating all the abuses of his regime. The letter is of the greatest severity, and is extant, though probably Louis XIV never saw it. It was, though, known to Mme. de Maintenon. Fénelon's pupil, the heir to the throne, unhappily died before he could inherit the crown of France, one of the many disappointments Fénelon had to bear.

Fénelon got into a furious quarrel with Bossuet over a Catholic mystical doctrine called *Quietism*, a belief that did not find the Church a necessary mediator between man and God. As a result of this quarrel, Fénelon was condemned by the Pope and banished to a provincial diocese. Fénelon became one of the more admired thinkers of the Seventeenth Century in the eyes of the Eighteenth Century Philosophes. The Philosophes ignored the fact that he believed in the divine right of kings, and in the place of the aristocracy in society, and that he was a devout Catholic. They exaggerated his Liberalism and made him a great protagonist of humanitarianism, of universal brotherhood, of optimism and progress, and of resistance to stupid royal authority. They even imagined Fénelon was a deist.

Fontenelle (d. 1757, one month before his hundredth birthday) had brilliant social gifts, and was a facile stylist able to charm the men and women of his time. He was educated by the Jesuits, and early in life became the lion of successive salons. His rapid advance was, in part, due to the efforts of his uncle, the dramatist, Pierre Corneille. Fontenelle became a social and intellectual celebrity before he was thirty. He was elected to the French Academy, and over sixty years served as secretary of the Academy of Sciences where his speeches praising recently deceased members form a sort of history of science during his long life.

Fontenelle's first important work was *Dialogues of the Dead*. Written in a witty style and with a good deal of cynicism, he presented a disillusioned picture of human frailties. In the quarrel of "Ancients" and "Moderns" he, in a spirited fashion, took the side of the "Moderns" and was their most effective advocate. One of Fontenelle's most successful and widely read books was that on the *Plurality of Worlds*. Presenting the universe as a machine like a watch, it popularized new scientific ideas and discoveries. Everything is made clear and is livened up with jokes and witty remarks. To avoid the censor he resorted often to wit, irony, and clever subterfuge, as Voltaire said later, to "strike and conceal your hand."

His *History of Oracles* attracted an even wider attention. Herein he shows the trickery of ancient priests and rulers and the amazing credulity of men. Indirectly, Fontenelle's book is leveled against all belief in the marvelous and the supernatural. Everywhere he seeks a rational and scientific explanation of things, and writes a powerful attack on human stupidity and gullibility.

Fontenelle performed no experiments, and published nothing new in science, but he knew all the scientific work of the Sixteenth and Seventeenth Centuries, and was well aware of the scientific discoveries of his own time. Fontenelle's *Thoughts on the Plurality of Worlds* was a brilliant popularization of the Copernican theory of the nature of the universe, together with a summary of later scientific work. With Fontenelle, the apostle of science and rationalism, science ceased to be the monopoly of experts and became part of the subject matter of general literature. He defended mechanical law in place of providence, and he helped to lead men away from Christianity and the Church to religious skepticism, and to an all-embracing faith in science. Fontenelle was original in introducing the idea of the sciences as intimately connected, as constituting a system on which the advance of one science will contribute to the advance of others. And his writing was free of technicalities and very lucid, and thus appealed not only to men of science but to the educated public at large. In his writings and in his conversation, Fontenelle represented direct and unprejudiced reason, unswayed by emotion; he was, indeed, the personified spirit of scientific rationalism. Fontenelle put the scientist in the niche that had formerly been reserved for the classical scholar or the artist in the Renaissance and by the saint in the Middle Ages. He created a kind of scientific and secular sainthood. Advances in the sciences were to overthrow mystical credulity and the abstract systems of the philosophers. This dislike of religion and of metaphysical philosophy and this faith in science clearly foreshadows the views of most of the Eighteenth Century Philosophes. Fontenelle's great admiration for science is well summed up in an often quoted remark, "the geometric spirit is not so much bound up with geometry that it cannot be carried into other fields. A work of morals, of politics, or of criticism will be the finer, other things being equal, if it is written by the hand of a geometer."

The sharpest French critic of the Age of Louis XIV, and a very important precursor of the Philosophes, was Pierre Bayle (d. 1706). He was the son of a Protestant pastor. The favorite authors of his youth were Plutarch and Montaigne. Bayle studied with the Jesuits and went to the University of Toulouse. He was, for a short time, converted to Catholicism, like Rousseau later. But he soon returned to Protestantism, and his father sent him to study in Geneva. Here he became deeply under the influence of the writings of Descartes. Later he taught in a Protestant academy at Sedan until the government closed the school. Next, he went into exile in Holland, and taught in an academy in Rotterdam until the French Protestants there forced him to resign his position because of his unorthodox opinions. While teaching at Sedan, he had published his *Thoughts on the Comet*. In this, Bayle showed that comets were natural phenomena and did not, as popularly believed, foretell disasters. He pointed out in passing that atheists are less dangerous than idolators, and that lack of religious faith does not necessarily lead to bad conduct. A society of atheists could be more moral than a society founded on religious superstition. The book attracted much attention, went through many editions, and made Bayle famous.

His next book, written in Holland, was a work on religious toleration, *Criticism of the History of Calvinism by Father Maimbourg*. It was full of moderation and reasonableness, and made a strong plea for toleration. The work attracted much attention, and was forbidden to be sold in France. He set forth the idea that religious ideas could not be forced on men and that individual conscience was the sole judge of right action. In the meantime, Bayle was editing a popular periodical, *News of the Republic of Letters.* It was widely read all over Europe, and spread the knowledge of new ideas in many fields.

Bayle wrote a strong attack on Louis XIV's revocation of the *Edict of Nantes* wherein he pointed out that such persecution leads only to skepticism or deism. In these earlier writings he condemned the religious traditions of both Catholics and Protestants, and, though he always remained a French Protestant, he preached a profound skepticism. Only the Bible, interpreted by individual conscience, should be followed. And he pointed out that men could lead a moral life without supernatural aid. "Nothing is more common," he wrote, "than to see orthodox Christians living evil lives, and free thinkers living good ones." Bayle rejected the idea that human nature was evil and needed a divine miracle to transform it. He also rejected the idea of original sin, emphasized the necessity of using reason to interpret the Bible, and believed a multiplicity of religions would be beneficial to the state. "It is enough," he wrote, "that every man consult sincerely and in good faith the light that God gives him and seize upon the idea that seems the most reasonable and most conformable to God's will."

Bayle was in his writings influenced by a current of Biblical criticism that had appeared in the Seventeenth Century. Colet, Erasmus, and a number of the northern Humanists of the Renaissance had laid great emphasis on reading the Bible rather than merely using it as an arsenal of quotations for Scholastic arguments. In the Seventeenth Century, a number of critics had gone further, and applied to the Bible, especially to the Old Testament, the methods of textual criticism being applied to secular documents. Among these criticisms, Simon's *Critical History of the Old Testament* of 1675 stands out. Simon applied methods of the criticism of secular documents to the Old Testament, and proved it had been corrupted by copyists, and showed the books supposedly written by Moses could not have been written by him as they contained contradictions and matter inserted after Moses' death. Simon went further and denied miracles as being against the scientific idea of the absolute regularity of nature. A little earlier Hobbes had criticized the popular views of the Old Testament. He easily proved that the first books were not written by Moses, that the Book of Joshua was written long after his time, that other books of the Old Testament were much later than the events they narrate, and that the Psalms were put in order after the return from Babylon. Many of the same ideas were held by Spinoza. So in his criticisms of the Bible, Bayle was not entirely an innovator.

In 1697 Bayle published his most important work, an *Historical and Critical Dictionary*. It was a great summary of skepticism that deftly undermined the foundations of the Seventeenth Century intellectual world. The articles, which deal chiefly with religion, history, and philosophy, were largely biographical about both religious and secular persons, though the dictionary also contained some topical articles. The amount and accuracy of the information is astounding. Believing that much evil had been caused by the veneration of persons who had not been worthy examples of morality, Bayle proceeded to try to get at the truth, saying that "it is of great importance that the lives of the orthodox be judged by the general actions of justice and order." Bayle submitted all ideas, facts, assumptions, and dogmas to a thorough examination. His three rules were 1) don't attack your opponents till you are sure of your arguments, 2) realize that "the proofs of feeling conclude nothing" if your object is to discover the truth, and 3) accept nothing without clear evidence. Often Bayle put the most damaging material into long footnotes, and he spent too much time on obscure figures while neglecting important ones. An example of his method is shown in his famous article on David. He showed that David had, in many ways, a bad character, that he was very sensual, and was treacherous and cruel, and that he murdered Uriah to get possession of Uriah's wife. The *Dictionary* was a subtle mixture of useful information and tendentious opinion. It probably did more than any other Seventeenth Century book to shake the yoke of authority. It was so well known to all the Philosophes of the Eighteenth Century that one critic called Bayle's *Dictionary* "the Bible of the Eighteenth Century."

So, all in all, the precursors of the Philosophes of the Eighteenth Century Enlightenment in France were those authors whose ideas and arguments could be used in the Philosophes' propaganda. The Philosophes were both derivative in their ideas and original in extending and amplifying old ideas, and both sides of their position in the history of thought must be emphasized. Of the Philosophes in general it may be said, as Mme. de Staël wrote of Rousseau, "He invented nothing but he set everything on fire."

2

THE NATURE
OF THE ENLIGHTENMENT
IN FRANCE

1. What was the French Enlightment?

The Enlightenment (called the Siècle des Lumières in French, and the Aufklärung in German) took a new world view; it involved the reevaluation of all values, established a new order of thought, and transformed the standards of humanity. The leaders doubted the validity of old religious, ethical, and political systems, and turned from otherworldly and pessimistic ideas to a secular view of life and an optimistic attitude toward the future. Knowledge took the place of grace, and the Philosophes appealed to all reasonable men to overthrow the ideas handed down from the past and to accept the rule of reason. Interest was centered now in this world, and life was made to be enjoyed. As the youthful revolutionary Saint-Just later put it, in a speech to the Convention, "Happiness is a new idea in Europe." The Philosophes set up new standards of truth based on standards of science and common sense. The Humanists of the Renaissance had set up the authority of classical writers and the leaders of the Reformation had referred all judgments to the Bible. But the Philosophes found their basis for truth in the laws of nature and the use of reason. Unlike the Renaissance Humanists and the reformers of the Reformation, who had found new and absolute standards of truth, a few of the Philosophes like Montesquieu doubted the existence of absolute standards.

Most of the Philosophes, however, believed in new but absolute standards which could be discovered by reason. "Consult your reason," wrote Chesterfield, "I do not say it will always prove an unerring guide, but it will prove the least erring guide that you can follow." "Dare to use your own understanding" wrote Kant, "this is the motto of Enlightenment." The leaders renounced the Christian ideas of the weakness of man's intellect and man's inherent sinfulness for the view that human nature was essentially good, provided it was guided by reason. The Philosophes fiercely attacked the power of old authority and of tradition. They believed that the human understanding is capable by its own power and without supernatural aid of knowing the nature and meaning of the world and of man, and of mastering nature, and, by the use of experiment and reason, of controlling the life of man.

One of the causes of these changes in the thought was the great growth of the middle classes. The older privileged orders, the monarchy, the aristocracy, and the Church, tended to cling to old ideas and values. The Philosophe had but one weapon—his ideas. Naturally he exalted them. The middle classes could now read, and had enough wealth to buy books, and they began to think about the new ideas spread by the

Philosophes. The Philosophes wrote primarily for the discontented middle classes. Economic conditions were growing better in Eighteenth Century France, at least for the more well-to-do classes, but many men felt they should improve more rapidly. And the middle classes objected strenuously to the privileges enjoyed by the nobility and the Church. The Philosophes were also much read outside of France for, by 1750, the French language, French ideas, and French manners had spread all over Europe, even to Russia, and to the Americas.

The masses, especially the overwhelming majority of them who were farmers, were little affected. That the masses were unaffected by the propaganda of the Philosophes is shown by their indifference and hostility to the Cults of Reason and of the Supreme Being set up by the Convention. In spite of the disaffection of many of the middle classes, the masses remained solidly Roman Catholic.

The Philosophes themselves for the most part lived on pensions granted by some of the nobility and by wealthy members of the middle class, and on the sale of their books which often gave them a substantial income.

The views of the Enlightenment were partly inherited piecemeal from the thinkers of earlier centuries, especially from those of the Seventeenth Century. But the Philosophes gave these ideas wider and more thoroughgoing application—investigating, criticizing, and reconstructing all sorts of ideas about religion, politics, education, psychology, and the arts. The fervor of the reformers seemed to be constructing "a new religion of which reason was God, Newton's ideas the Bible,

Voltaire and others the prophets." The Philosophes attempted to offer the spiritual leadership of which, they believed, the Church was no longer capable. These reformers put forth a huge propaganda in books, pamphlets, articles, and journals, and in a vast *Encyclopedia*, all full of serious reasoning and of witty mockery.

Reason would unlock all the secrets of the universe, and would correct the rules for running both society and individual conduct. The Philosophes were eminently practical and utilitarian, and aimed to promote happiness and well-being among all classes. Among the first principles of the Philosophes were the following: the only justification for the State is for the promotion of the good life for its citizens, men should be rational, they can conceive the good, can discover means of obtaining it, and should be allowed, if they used reason, to direct their own lives by their knowledge, reason, and experience. The ability to use their reason makes men equal, laws should accord with popular wishes and should preserve men's rights, and with the use of reason, progress is sure to come. They were also optimistic about the chances of reforming everything and of building a better future. No longer would Scholastic traditions, the authority of Church and state, nor the sanctity of revelation bar the rule of experiment and reason.

The reign of Louis XV was a failure and the administration seemed to be going to pieces. Disastrous wars led to the loss of great possessions. A patriotic Frenchman might well have despaired of the present and the future. But hopefulness was in the air. "In order to regret the past," wrote one critic in 1772, "one must be ignorant of what it was." "We had no regret for the past," wrote another, "and no inquietude for the future. We believed that we were entering a golden age; we were the disciples of new doctrines, the prejudices of old customs seemed absurd. Voltaire charmed our intelligence, and Rousseau touched our hearts."

Everywhere the reformers believed there was a natural order of things to which men and institutions should conform. There was a natural law, a natural ethics, a natural economy, and a natural religion, though the Philosophes differed among themselves in trying to define these natural systems. The Philosophes did not discover the rights of man, but they made these rights the foundation of an ethical and social gospel which they strove vigorously and hopefully to introduce into practical affairs.

In order to discover the secrets of nature and of man's behavior they demanded freedom of thought. They also were openly at war with all that was irrational especially as the irrational was found in religion and popular superstitions. In the name of humanity, they attacked the penal codes. Some of the Philosophes believed in some form of benevolent despotism for it could most effectively and quickly promote thorough-going reforms. Democracy was looked on with less favor because of its lack of experience, its tendency to go to extremes, and because it often meant the rule of the irrational. The Philosophes were especially critical of traditional religion. They regarded the Church as intolerant and as sunk in superstition. The claims of each church to be the exclusive means of salvation disgusted them. The faith in revelation, in miracles, in dogmas, and in sacraments aroused their special ire.

At first glance the ideas of the Philosophes might appear to be an uncoordinated collection of high-minded Liberal sentiments, almost platitudes today. Yet the common ideas of one age were once the novel discoveries of an earlier generation. It is easy today to overlook the fact that the Philosophes spread among a great number of the literate population of the Eighteenth Century, a new view of the world that was radically at variance with the accepted views of the Middle Ages and of the Reformation Era. So successful were they that at bottom we are still the spiritual children of the Eighteenth Century. This is shown in the fact that we still believe that man and his institutions can be changed, that social and political problems can be improved rather than endured, that the goal of human life is maximum self-realization here below, and that the future is a challenge and an opportunity. The ideas of the Enlightenment were thus by no means platitudinous in their time. They have come to seem so, paradoxically because of their key power to make converts.

The traditional Christian God was obviously too willful and capricious to have been the creator of Newton's orderly world machine, and so He was rejected in favor of a deistic God as the first cause and prime mover, or of no God at all. Likewise the traditional Christian view of man as tainted by original sin, enduring this vale of tears, and hoping for salvation was no longer acceptable, at least in the old form. All in all, the reasonable course for man seemed to be to forget about sin in the old sense, and to concentrate on his self-development here and now. There appeared to be plenty of room for reform. And the Philosophes demanded reforms that would make man's institutions as harmonious and logically balanced as the movement of the celestial bodies; man's laws should be as rational as those of physics. The Philosophes differed in what they singled out for criticism; they seldom conducted their criticism in a systematic fashion, and they did not always agree on the proper solutions to problems. But beneath this superficial diversity of opinions, there lay always a common assumption that institutions exist for man rather than the reverse, and that all institutions must justify their existence on the basis of utility rather than of antiquity.

In their writings, the reformers strove for clarity and readability, and they had much recourse to irony and wit. Eloquence, emotion, and profundity were not for them, except on rare occasions. They wanted to be read and understood by all sorts and conditions of men. In their prose writings, the Philosophes broke down the old-fashioned, elaborate and Ciceronian periods, and discarded similes, metaphors, and imagery. They strove to strip the idea of everything that was not of its essence, and to eliminate all vagueness and decoration. They aimed at being vital, direct, and rapid. On the other hand, the Age of Enlightenment was signally lacking in the writing of great poetry. One historian says "What makes the Enlightenment vie with the Hellenization of the world after Alexander, with the conquest of the west by Roman law and language, with the propagation of Christianity, with the Renaissance and the Reformation as a turning point in civilization is less the wonderful new ideas which it originated than the energy with which it diffused these ideas. With an intensity of conviction almost religious, with a missionary zeal for the conversion of the masses, a chosen band of apostles set out to educate the public in the principles which, they believed, would prove as efficacious in the amelioration of the lot of mankind as they had been effective in explaining the operations of nature."

The name that the Philosophes took for themselves does not mean philosophers in the ordinary sense. They avoided and disliked metaphysics and all abstract systems of thought. "The Philosophe," said one writer, "does not count himself an exile in the world, he would fain find pleasure with others. He is a worthy man who wishes to please and to make himself useful. The ordinary philosophers, who meditate too much, are as surly and arrogant to all the world as great people are to those whom they do not think their equals; they flee men and men avoid them. But our Philosophe, who knows how to divide himself between retreat and the commerce of men is full of humanity. Civil society is a divinity for him on earth. He honors it by an exact attention to his duties, and by a sincere desire not to be useless." Another writer defined a "Philosophe" as "one who applies himself to the study of society with the purpose of making his kind better and happier."

The Philosophes were primarily propagandists and publicists anxious for both thorough-going and peaceful reform. The writers of the Enlightenment strongly felt that theirs was a new and enlightened age, and it is from their own evaluation of themselves that the age takes its name. They were convinced that Europe was, at last, emerging from a long twilight, a long period when nearly everything was now regarded as barbarous and murky. The Philosophes were not an organized party though they tended—with the exception of Rousseau—to have a party line. And even Rousseau agreed with many of the ideas of the other Philosophes. They were a party with a left wing, a center, and a right wing, but still a party. They were drawn together by common enemies of Church and state. Sometimes they quarreled among themselves as members of a party will. Holbach and Rousseau attacked Helvétius' idea of the selfishness of man. Voltaire hounded all who disagreed with him, and d'Alembert, who opposed censorship, wanted the censors to suppress the writings of his opponents! The temperaments were varied, but they were almost all very French in their passion for logical clarity, and they agreed in more respects than they disagreed. Especially did many of the Philosophes dislike Rousseau. In their enthusiasm and fervor, a Philosophe might call those who disagreed with him scoundrels and bigots.

Nearly all the Philosophes studied some branch of science, as did many monarchs, aristocrats, and wealthy bourgeois. Voltaire talked of devoting his life to the study of chemistry, and he worked hard and long to understand and spread Newtonian physics. Some of Montesquieu's first publications were scientific. D'Alembert was a physicist and a mathematician. Diderot dabbled in all the sciences, and Rousseau wrote a botanical dictionary. Louis XV had scientific collections, just as George III specialized in botany, the King of Portugal in astronomy, and the King of Piedmont in physics. The press and journals were full of reviews of works on science, and a flood of books was published on every aspect of science. The first four decades of the Eighteenth Century are strongly rationalist in outlook and much under the influence of science. After 1750 the claims of reason and science began somewhat to fade before the imperative demands of sentiment and emotion, and the demand for practical reforms. Though in both periods there is a continuing attack on the institutions of the Ancien Régime, political, religious, social, and economic. The Enlightenment thus evolved and did not remain static.

The Age of Enlightenment was also marked by a great growth of humanitarianism. Reason saw the futility and cruelty of vindictive penalties and of oppression. The Church had laid emphasis on the joys of a life hereafter, and had held that earthly suffering is beneficial to the soul even though the Church had always undertaken great programs of charity to contribute to earthly comforts. But when the vision of a future life began to fade, the pleasures and woes of this life assumed greater importance. The gradual elevation of the masses made men more aware of social misery, and the increase of wealth of the middle classes furnished the means of extending philanthropy. Writers joined now to acclaim the worth and the misery of the masses, and many agreed with Franklin that a virtuous plowman is worth more than a vicious prince, and that a man should be valued for his own worth and not for that of his ancestors. Gray, in his *Elegy*, expressed admirably the new wave of humanitarianism that swept the Eighteenth Century.

"Let not Ambition mock their useful toil
Their homely joys and destiny obscure,
Nor Grandeur hear with a disdainful smile
The short and simple annals of the poor."

The propaganda of the Enlightenment was both negative and positive. On the negative side, the Philosophes were largely in accord in denouncing both the present and the past. In both they could find a few enlightened souls, but mostly they denounced furiously the abuses and superstitions they found in the story of the past and in the life of the present. Their books were filled with idol smashing. On the positive side, their propaganda represented wave after wave of positive faith in ideas that would remake the future. First, they had faith in man if he were ruled by reason. The majority of the Philosophes centered their faith in man in his reason, but with Rousseau the faith in reason was combined with a faith in emotion. As we have seen, they also had great faith that science, when applied, would improve the condition of man in this world. Great was the faith of some of the Philosophes in progress and in the future of mankind. They had great faith likewise in various kinds of freedom: political freedom, intellectual and religious freedom, economic freedom, national freedom (of which the greatest champion was the German,

Herder), and, in the later Eighteenth Century, in freedom in all the arts: literature, art, and music. All in all, the Philosophes were more marked by their tremendous upsurges of faith than they were by their iconoclastic and negative criticisms of the past and the present.

The allegiance of the Philosophes to reason was a noble and immensely beneficent thing; to try all ideas and institutions by the light of the best science and thought of the time was better than to accept blindly ancient abuses and absurdities that had come down from previous centuries. As one critic writes, "To Voltaire and his fellows we owe it that abuses were attacked, cruelties exposed, and absurdities shown to be such. The cloud of superstition that had darkened the Middle Ages and which later burst in a devastating storm of persecution and religious wars was rolled away." In addition, the Philosophes either founded or deeply affected all the social sciences: government, history, economics, sociology, and psychology.

Nor was their victory easily won. Against them were all the vested interests of an old society. Diderot's works were suppressed, and he was imprisoned. Buffon had to retract his ideas on geology, Voltaire was twice imprisoned in the Bastille, and was forced to live much of his life in exile from France. Others had their books condemned, and few of the Philosophes were without disagreeable conflicts with the law. Brutal edicts condemned publishers and book-sellers to the galleys or to death. But with all the weapons in the hands of their enemies, the Philosophes won a great victory in the minds of the middle class and some of the aristocracy.

The Philosophes were, from a Twentieth Century point of view, more conservative than they realized. In religion, their deism was a cautious compromise, and those who were atheists were never sure of themselves. In their ideas, few had the modern notion of the relativity of truth. They wanted reforms, not a revolution, and few had faith in democracy. They believed in progress through the use of reason and the spread of education, but they did not arrive at the idea of the evolution of man and his institutions. Most of their scientific ideas were to be outmoded by the scientific discoveries of succeeding centuries.

The Philosophes were frequently guilty of hasty and unfounded generalizations, of incomplete analyses, and of a nebulous and naive optimism. Anything not easily understood was dismissed as pedantry, and metaphysics was rejected because it raised questions that were essentially unanswerable and were beyond the ken of reason. It was better to devote one's thought to practical matters than to indulge in vague speculation. The salons, the press, and the reading public demanded striking literary effects and epigrams, but these were not conducive to patient research and sober generalizations. Also the Philosophes tried vainly to reduce humanity to physics, and to make man and society into Newtonian machines. Burke early saw these shortcomings when he wrote "the lines of morality are not like the lines of mathematics. They are broad and deep as well as long; they admit exceptions; they demand modifications. These exceptions and modifications are not made by the process of logic but by the rule of prudence." In a word, the Philosophes ignored the fact, as John Adams said of man in general, "he is a reasoning but not a reasonable animal!"

2. The Spread of New Ideas

The spread of new ideas is as important to the historian of culture as the creation of these ideas. If the theories of the Philosophes had been limited to a relatively small number of readers, as were for example those of Spinoza, they would never have created the revolution in thinking that was their accomplishment. To their own way of thinking, the Philosophes were freethinkers who set out to change the minds of large numbers of men. Their purposes were definitely practical, and they vowed to apply to man's institutions the force of reason. What did not fit into their programs was ignored or ridiculed. Their attacks on old ideas and their positive programs of reform attracted the interest and attention of thousands of readers, and they became the darlings of a large part of the reading public. The currents of Liberal thought gathered strength as the Eighteenth Century proceeded. In the first half of the Eighteenth Century Hume had blamed the Seventeenth Century for dividing the elegant part of mankind into two widely divided parts, the profound thinkers and the reading public, and he lauded his own century for uniting both parts to the advantage of each section. It was Kant who invented the word Aufklärung for this new age that was leading "the liberation of man from his self-imposed minority."

Various means were used to spread the new ideas. The salon had been an invention of the Seventeenth Century. Now in the Eighteenth Century the salons both in Paris and in some of the provinces were captured by the purveyors of new and radical ideas as were also some of the provincial academies. In the salons conversation was clever and sparkling even though it was often superficial. The Philosophes learned to make all ideas clear. The leaders of the salons were mostly women, such as Mme. de Tencin, Mme. Geoffrin, Mme. Necker, and, above all others, Mme. du Deffand and Mlle. de Lespinasse.

Each of these great ladies was herself a wit. When a bishop told Mme. du Deffand that St. Denis, after having been beheaded on Montmartre, carried his head in his hand twelve kilometers before he lay down to die, she replied, "In a circumstance like that it is the first step that counts!" It was often the custom of the Philosophes to attend several salons in turn. It was an age of talk. Someone asked Diderot if he had read the Abbé Raynal. "No," he answered, "because I have neither the time nor the taste for reading. To read all alone without having anyone to talk to, and with whom to agree and to listen, or to be listened to, that is impossible." A great variety of subjects were discussed: politics, religion, education, art, science, business and agriculture, literature, music, and the theater. The talk flowed freely among the visitors in the salons, which included noblemen, wealthy bourgeois, government officials, and men outstanding in literature, science, art, and music. In the salons, the Philosophes dictated taste and ideas. Even those who had secure incomes depended on the salon for full success. The future of a book was often subject to its reception in some drawing room, and election to the French Academy was usually dependent on intrigues in the salons.

This sort of patronage often did corrupt the Philosophes. "Women," said Diderot, "accustom us to discuss with charm and clarity the driest and thorniest subjects. We talk to them unceasingly. We wish them to listen; we are afraid of tiring or boring them; hence we develop a particular method of explaining ourselves easily, and this passes from conversation into style" (of writing). The Philosophe was forced to adjust his style to please his hostess. Horace Walpole, in his letters, complains that the salons spoiled the Philosophes whom he found overbearing and wearisome. Walpole may have had an aristocratic prejudice against bourgeois men of letters and wealthy bourgeois businessmen who were admitted to social intimacy with the nobility to an extent that was not found in any other European country. Many of the best books written by the Philosophes were composed away from the salon. Montesquieu declared, "My great work now advances with gigantic studies since I am no longer harassed with Parisian invitations to toilsome dinners and fatiguing suppers." Voltaire's best books were written away from Paris, and Rousseau early learned that the salons were not for him.

Some men, especially wealthy men, held salons where the conversation was more serious though no less witty. Most famous of these salons was that of Baron d'Holbach, known as "the personal enemy of the Almighty." The guests, who were all men, met at two. It was often seven before they dispersed, and there was no question that did not come under discussion. It was, says Holbach, "the most free, the most animated, and most instructive conversation that it was ever possible to hear." Here, at Baron d'Holbach's table, one might meet the unkempt and eloquent Diderot, Buffon, Turgot, Rousseau, and the young Condorcet, and foreign celebrities like Hume, Wilkes, Garrick, Franklin, and Priestly. After 1760, the growing vogue of the writing of Rousseau gave the salons new subjects for discussion; sentimentalism and politics were slowly taking the place of skepticism and philosophy. The judgment of the court had been decisive in the Seventeenth Century France in all matters of art, literature, and general ideas, but in the Eighteenth Century this center of influence had been transferred to Paris, and especially to the salons of Paris.

Besides the salons, coffee houses, cafes, clubs, and public lending libraries played a great role in disseminating the ideas of the Philosophes. Some clubs were formed to drink coffee and punch and beer, to smoke, and exchange ideas openly. Others were secret, and, more or less in a spirit of conspiracy, propagated Liberal religious and political ideas. The largest of these secret societies was that of the Free-Masons, founded in London in 1717. The society spread with amazing rapidity. The first lodge was established in Paris in 1725, and others soon afterwards appeared in all the European states including Russia. Some of the lodges maintained libraries, and the Free-Masonic lodges were important in the spread of new ideas.

The fact that the Free-Masons were usually deist, and were favorable to the reforming ideas of the Philosophes has led a few historians, wrongly, to make out that the French Revolution was due to a Masonic plot against the Ancien Régime.

Magazines, newspapers, and books also reached a wide circle of readers through the public libraries kept by the state and through privately owned circulating libraries. These helped to spread the new ideas of the Philosophes to a large public. The periodical press was mostly hostile to the Philosophes and their ideas, but the period produced no writer of much ability to oppose the Philosophes. The most widely read books were novels and text books, and the journals and newspapers talked, as one historian says, mostly "of harvests, gout, chicken, prices, and gossip" and only rarely of the Philosophes. How large was the reading public of the Philosophes it is not possible to say. Frederick the Great estimated that two hundred thousand people in all Europe read Voltaire. Seven editions of the *Encyclopedia* were sold out before the end of the Eighteenth Century; there were nineteen editions of the complete works of Voltaire between 1740 and his death in 1778, and a much larger number of editions of some of Voltaire's single works, such as *Candide*. Eighteen editions of Rousseau's writings appeared before 1789, and over fifty editions of his *New Heloise.* But nearly all changes in thought have been the work of minorities, and if there were two hundred thousand readers of the Philosophes in Europe, this would account for the revolution in thought which they caused.

Censorship, in theory at least, was very strict. But its enforcement was whimsical and unpredictable. One work might be suppressed and another that could have been considered equally dangerous was allowed to be printed and circulated. In one of his plays, Beaumarchais makes the character, Figaro, say, "Provided I do not write anything about religion, politics, morality, or officials, I am at liberty to print what I choose—under the inspection of two or three censors." All new works were first required to be passed by a state censor. But that often did not end the matter, for on protest of another government department, or of the Sorbonne, or of the Parlement of Paris, or of the Church, the work might suddenly be withdrawn from circulation. Government penalties were often severe on the author, the publishers and the book-seller. Many were sent to prison and some to the galleys.

Authors, publishers, and book-sellers devised various means of circumventing the authorities. Authors sometimes published anonymously or under a pseudonym. Fearful of criticizing directly, authors threw their criticism onto an abstract level. Debarred from attacking things in particular, they attacked things in general or talked about the Persians and the Iroquois when they meant the French. They became expert in the use of double meanings, of sly digs, innuendos, sarcasms, and jokes. There were few Philosophes who escaped the rigor of the laws, but they were not silenced. The censorship was irritating but not efficacious. Helvètius well expressed the exasperation of the Philosophes with censorship when he wrote, "Most governments urge their citizens to search for truth; but almost all governments punish them for finding it." Some books were published in Holland or, more rarely in England or Switzerland, and smuggled into France. Others were printed in France with the name of a foreign city on the title page. Many books were published secretly in Paris or the provinces. There was an extensive clandestine sale and circulation of forbidden books, both in manuscript and printed form. Book-sellers would secretly sell censored books to customers they trusted, and there was a great deal of passing of forbidden books from one friend to another. In some degree the Philosophes profited by the censorship, for word in the press that the public hangman had been ordered to burn a book made some of the public anxious to read the book, and so acted as an advertisement.

3

MONTESQUIEU

1. His Earlier Life and Work.

Montesquieu (1689-1755) was the first Philosophe to win a widespread reputation. He was the son of a member of the nobility of the robe, and, as a youth, he received a good education with emphasis on Latin and historical studies. Montesquieu then took a degree in law at the University of Bordeaux. After this he went for a time to Paris where his interest centered in scientific studies, and where he met Fontenelle and other scholars including some who were specialists in classical history and Chinese studies. On his return to Bordeaux he inherited the presidency of the Parlement of Bordeaux. Though he was a Catholic with deistic leanings, he married a wealthy Protestant heiress, and soon inherited a good deal of property from his father and uncle. He was now a well-to-do man, but, later, he always lived beyond his means, and was often in debt.

Elected to membership in the Academy of Bordeaux, his early papers were on Roman religion in which he shows the influence of Machiavelli and of Bayle. Montesquieu soon became the director of the Academy which laid emphasis on scientific experiments and on independence of judgment. Among his publications, connected with the Academy, were some on

50

scientific experiments in biology. He observed under the microscope the effect of cold in contracting and of heat in expanding animal tissue. From these experiments, he deduced that differences in climate had a profound influence on people, and helped to form national characteristics. Also from science he drew the idea that human institutions should be examined from an experimental and objective point of view. Early in life Montesquieu's reason and scholarly interests overrode his class interest as a nobleman.

While still living in his family chateau near Bordeaux, he started to write his *Persian Letters*, which was published anonymously in 1721, in Holland, but with Cologne on the title page. The work at once enjoyed a great success, and went through ten editions in one year. It tells the story, in letters, of two Persians whom he imagines travelling in Western Europe, spending most of their time in France. They write home impressions of what they see and hear. Montesquieu also included supposed letters from the wives and eunuchs of one of the Persians. Travel letters had earlier been popularized by explorers and missionaries, and interest in the Middle East had just been stimulated by a new translation of the *Koran* and the *Arabian Nights*.

Montesquieu's description of customs in the Middle East are said, by scholars, to be surprisingly accurate, and shows that the author had studied carefully the literature available on the subject. The two young Persians comment on the political events and manners of the time, especially what they supposedly saw in Paris. As with Rabelais, nothing is spared.

It is interesting to see that, although Montesquieu is a sharp critic of conditions in France, he insists on relative standards of morality, politics, and religion. The range of subjects covered is very wide.

Montesquieu expresses his belief in God, but is very critical of the Church. The Pope, he declares, is a magician who teaches that three and one are the same things, and that bread is not bread and wine is not wine. The Pope, he declares, is an old idol worshipped through force of habit. His comment on most religious institutions and practices is one of skepticism and disrespect. Montesquieu believed strongly in religious toleration, and declared that it is morality and not faith that is important. The best way to please God is by observing the rules of society and the duties of humanity. Compared with these obligations, the practices, rules, and ceremonies of all religions are insignificant.

On religious toleration he wrote, "All prejudice aside, I do not know if it is not a good thing to have several religions in a state. Besides, since all religions entertain some useful precepts, it is good to have them zealously observed, and what is more apt than a multiplicity of religions to inspire zeal? It has always been observed that the introduction of a new sect into a state has been the surest means of correcting the abuses of the older sect." All this is part of Montesquieu's attack on Louis XIV's revocation of the *Edict of Nantes* and the large amount of religious persecution that still prevailed in France. He is also very critical of celibacy and monasticism, on which he blames the decline of population in France.

The principal aim of the *Letters* is to destroy prejudice. Throughout the book reigns the idea that man, thanks to the use of reason, can free himself from prejudice. He attacks absolute monarchy as he attacks the Church. The King of France is another magician. The King of France can get men to kill each other when they have no actual quarrel with anyone. Only magic could make men behave so irrationally. Magic seems also to possess inquisitors, who are "a species of dervish who burn those who differ from them on mere trivialities." By contrast, Montesquieu praises the government and society of England where parliamentary government and toleration prevails. He declares that the King in France should rule not for his personal glory, as the recently deceased Louis XIV had, but for the welfare of his people. Montesquieu also vigorously attacks slavery which Christians, when it suited their economic interests, still maintain. He, likewise, has advanced views on women. The sexes should be equal "if they have equal opportunities for education." Also he is opposed to foreign colonies because, he maintains, they draw economic strength away from the mother country. Montesquieu classified governments as monarchies, despotisms and republics. The first was appropriate for states of moderate size, the second for very large states, and the third for small states. This classification was to be repeated and extended later in his *Spirit of the Laws.*

Throughout Montesquieu's *Persian Letters*, the tone is witty and bantering, but underneath he is serious. Every few letters contain a risqué story to carry on the reader's attention.

A few years later Voltaire expressed surprise at the boldness of the *Persian Letters* and the fact that their author had been so little molested by the government. Actually, the *Letters* reflect the relief felt after the death of Louis XIV in 1715, and the gay, skeptical, and relaxed spirit of the rule of the Regent, the Duke of Orleans, whose reaction against the type of rule of Louis XIV was nearly complete. An atmosphere of independence and of bold criticisms of abuses was now abroad in the land. So the *Persian Letters* heralded the coming of a new age.

The publication of the *Persian Letters*, although they had been issued anonymously, attracted public attention to Montesquieu, and made him famous. He began now to spend long periods in Paris when he was received at the court of the Regent, and in some of the great houses and salons of the capital. Here Montesquieu, quick to learn, discovered many things about the government of France and the life of nobility. He also saw many of the leading intellectuals of the time, including Fontenelle and the Abbé de Saint-Pierre. He was received as a member of the famous *Club of the Entresol*, the first society in Paris for the free discussion of ideas. Montesquieu's chief interest seems to have centered in ideas on history, law, and government. In the meantime, he continued to present papers to the Academy of Bordeaux and had been elected to the French Academy.

Greatly interested not only in France but also in foreign lands, Montesquieu set out on four years of travel and foreign residence. The longest periods were spent in Italy and England, but he also visited Vienna, some of the German states, Holland, and Switzerland. Everywhere his fame as an author preceded him, and through this advance reputation and his status as a nobleman, he was able to meet the leading statesmen and intellectuals. In Italy, he probably met Vico, and he certainly came to know many of the leading scholars, especially those interested in Roman history. In England, he was elected to the Royal Society, initiated into Free-Masonry, read the current newspapers, visited sessions of Parliament to hear the debates, and met the leading men in politics and literature, probably including Pope. He had some acquaintance with the English language before he went to Britain, and he rapidly improved his speaking and reading knowledge of English. He had already met King George when in Hanover, and he was cordially received at the royal court in London. Montesquieu had earlier, in 1726, sold his position as President of the Parlement of Bordeaux, and so was now free to live where he pleased. For the rest of his life, he lived on the income of his estate, and devoted himself to study and writing.

After four years of travel and residence abroad, Montesquieu returned to his family estate near Bordeaux. The first result of his leisure was a number of short works and his *Considerations on the Causes of the Grandeur of the Romans and their Decadence* which was published anonymously at Amsterdam in 1734. Montesquieu had been interested in Roman history since his schooldays, and although less was known about the history of Rome in the Eighteenth Century than is known in the Twentieth Century, he seems to have read widely in the then existing literature. The Eighteenth Century liked to make comparisons between Roman history and the conditions existing in Europe at a later time. Montesquieu rejects Bossuet's belief in providence, and tries to confine himself to facts. He was not interested in telling again the story of Roman history, but rather in trying to discover its underlying significance. Behind his inquiry was always the question whether France after the blunders of Louis XIV and the debauched Regent, the Duke of Orleans, and the indifference of the cynical Louis XV could learn timely lessons from Rome's greatness and fall.

Montesquieu listed several factors that contributed to the greatness of the Roman Republic. First was the character of the Roman armies, made up largely of small, free-holding farmers who were allowed to share in the booty of conquests. A second reason for success was the unusual ability of the Romans to learn from their enemies and from the conquered peoples. Third, the government could be modified to correct abuses. Fourth was the wise policy of rewarding her allies and punishing her enemies; by this means they set one nation against another and one party among their enemies against another party. Last but not least was a great series of statesmen and rulers.

The causes of the decline of Rome he found to be numerous. The Empire became so large that the provinces lost contact with the capital, and forces in the frontiers were loyal only to their own commanders. Second, the great influx of foreigners who were not loyal to the government of Rome weakened the state. Then, the combining of small farms into large estates deprived the army of what had once been its backbone—i.e. the presence of free-holding soldiers. The Romans were no longer willing or very fit to serve in the army and fight in their own defense, but left this task to hired soldiers from among the barbarian immigrants. Next, Montesquieu noted the unhealthy growth of wealth and a corruption of morals due to this increase, and to a decline of traditional religion, and the growth of Epicureanism. The final downfall of Rome was due to the fact that the Europe in the West was attacked at once by many enemies, at a time when the state had been divided into Eastern and Western halves. A further cause of growing weakness Montesquieu also noted was that Christianity sapped the military and civic virtues of the Romans.

The Eastern Empire survived a thousand years longer than the Western Empire because of the lucrative commerce it commanded, its use of Greek fire, and the help given by the Crusades. The chief weaknesses of his whole account lay in his ignoring archeological evidence and of economic causes for the decline of Rome. Like Machiavelli and the writers of the Renaissance, Montesquieu assumed the accuracy and sufficiency of the ancient Roman historians, and made their works the basis of his interpretation of Roman affairs. The work, nonetheless, was very original, and long had an influence on the writing of Roman history. Gibbon, for example, drew many of his ideas from Montesquieu's work when writing *The Decline and Fall of the Roman Empire.* "My delight," wrote Gibbon later, "was in the frequent perusal of Montesquieu whose energy of style and boldness of hypothesis were powerful to awaken and stimulate the genius of the age." In his great work, Gibbon frequently quotes or refers to Montesquieu. He might disagree with Montesquieu, but he has him constantly in mind, and Gibbon's analyses of the reasons for Rome's fall are similar to those of Montesquieu. Part of the success of Montesquieu's writing is due to its excellent style; he handled the French language with consummate skill and clarity. As Voltaire said, Montesquieu "always thinks and makes others think."

2. The Spirit of the Laws

Montesquieu was now a well-known author. He still continued to manage his estate, but he also spent much time in Paris. Here he was frequently at meetings of the French Academy, and circulated freely in the salons where he saw his old friends Fontenelle and the Abbé de Saint-Pierre, and where he met Voltaire, Helvétius, and perhaps Rousseau. He himself entertained a great deal and his guests included distinguished foreigners, among whom were quite a number from Britain. Montesquieu's fame spread outside France, and he was elected to the Academy in Berlin. At the same time, he occasionally read papers, mostly on scientific subjects, to the Academy of Bordeaux. Through his reading, which was very extensive, and through a multitude of personal contacts he learned much about French and foreign politics and institutions.

Montesquieu worked for over twenty years on his master-

piece, *The Spirit of the Laws*, which was published anonymously in Geneva in 1748, and of which more than twenty
editions appeared in a year and a half. It was at once widely
read. The chapters are short, and it is easy to read. But it had
cost the author much trouble. "I have," he wrote, "begun
many times and many times abandoned this work." Despite
its rather ambiguous title it was a treatise on comparative government. His aim was far higher than his achievement. He
was trying to analyze the laws operating in social life, to build
up politics, morals, religion, and economics with all their rela-
tionships into a vast sociological synthesis, to reduce to scientific terms the social behavior of man. The task was far beyond
the possibilities of his time.

The work is hardly a systematic treatise on politics but a
book of disconnected reflexions. It is all in all a rather sprawl-
ing compilation drawn from ancient texts, contemporary explorers and writers, and his own observations. It often seems
to lack shape and organization. The generalizations on Far
Eastern governments, which Montesquieu did not know first-
hand, are one of the weakest things in the work. In spite of his
shortcomings, Montesquieu was almost the only Philosophe
who really tried to apply a scientific technique to social and
political problems.

Montesquieu was not merely concerned with the laws as
they were but as they ought to be. He said, though, "I do not
justify customs, I give reasons for them." He showed his Liberalism by taking thrusts at despotism, slavery, intolerance,
arbitrary taxation, and inhuman penal codes, and by praising

the Liberal institutions of England. However, he remained too objective, and too relative in his standards to suit the later Philosophes who found him too little committed to Liberal ideals. Almost alone among the Philosophes he realized that political and social problems are highly complex.

Montesquieu's work marks the passing for the time being of the well-worn idea of the social contract which was to be revived by Rousseau. In general, he believed that conditions and institutions were relative depending on the climate and soil, on the size of the state, and on its previous history. What was suited to man in certain climates and situations might very well be unsuited to the situation in other states. Condorcet said, "Montesquieu would have done better if he had not been more active with finding the reasons for that which is than with seeking that which ought to be." Montesquieu's treatise was written under a despotism by a man with limited experience of government and small possibility of such experience. His philosophy is a bookish one written for the educated middle classes. It abounds in formulas and sweeping generalizations. He strives after brilliant effects; Mme. du Deffand spoke of the *Spirit of the Laws* as "wit on the subject of laws." But the book managed to give comfort to reactionaries who hoped for the restoration of the Parlements and to Liberals who wanted to introduce an imitation of the English government.

Montesquieu begins with praise of the law of nature. Nature provides a standard of absolute justice prior to positive law. But this natural law, which he identified with reason, operated differently in different environments, and produced different institutions in different places. Climate, soil, occupations, forms of government, commerce, religion, and customs are all important conditions of what sort of government will prevail. Evidently he drew some of these ideas from Aristotle's *Politics* especially those parts which analyzed the different kinds of democracy, oligarchy, and despotism. His idea of the influence of climate on government came partly from Bodin.

Governments, according to Montesquieu, were of three kinds: republican fit only for small states, and dependent on civic virtue, i.e. the preference of the interest of one's country to one's self-interest; despotic, best fitted for large states, and dependent on fear; and monarchical, suited best to states of moderate size, and dependent on the sense of honor of a military class and on respect for law. His best examples of a republic are Athens, Sparta, and the Roman Republic; of despotism, the France of Richelieu and Louis XIV; and his best example of monarchy is England. Montesquieu goes into great detail about the organization of various types of government and the possible changes that may take place in these governments. He moves through an almost limitless diversity of morals, customs, laws, and institutions. He was trying to proceed from isolated facts and diversity to an intelligible order. Behind this diversity of facts, then, are underlying causes and rules which he tries to discover. Montesquieu's contribution was to combine the description of forms of government in such a way that each regime is also seen as a certain type of society.

In so far as the *Spirit of the Laws* has any plan, it consists in following out the changes in government required by circumstances. The first three books are introductory and are on forms of government. Books IV to X deal with educational institutions, criminal law, sumptuary laws, and the position of women with, as usual, many somewhat irrelevant matters thrown in. Books XI and XII discuss political and civil liberty; Book XIII deals with taxation. Books XIV to XVII are concerned with the influence of climate and soil on government and industry and their relation to slavery and political freedom. The argument from climate is very vaguely handled. He relates London fogs to the British Constitution and to religion in Britain! He declares that liberty is found in cold countries because the people are energetic, while despotism and slavery thrive in hot countries because the people are lazy. Even religions depend on the climate. Christianity is suitable to a cool climate; Mohammedanism flourishes in hot countries because it allows polygamy and slavery. In Europe, the Northern Countries became Protestant because it suited the independent spirit of the people; Southern Europe clung to Catholicism because they found it an easy and sensuous cult. His theories about climate are perhaps the weakest part of his argument, but they shared their weakness with other early Eighteenth Century literature on the same subjects which Montesquieu had read and used.

Book XVIII is devoted to effects of soil; Book XIX is concerned with the nebulous influence of customs; Books XX to XXII are observations on commerce and money; Book XXIII is on population, and the last two books are concerned with Roman and feudal law. Throughout, the author, though very learned, is addicted to hasty generalizations.

Perhaps the most positive and influential thing in this diffuse discussion was Montesquieu's praise of English institutions. He ascribed English freedom to the separation of powers in the government into executive, legislative, and judicial branches. There was no sovereign except the law, and the rule of law was maintained because authority was divided; each of the three functions of government was given just the requisite power to prevent the other functions from being abused. He failed to understand the developing cabinet system, and so did not see that the monarch was largely a figurehead, and that the executive power was actually in the hands of the Prime Minister and the Cabinet who were a part of the legislative branch of the government. The English government seemed to him the best because it offered the maximum of freedom and of security, and this arose because the various departments of the government mutually limited and controlled one another. What Montesquieu did not see was that personal rights in England were limited because the landlords, not the people, dominated Parliament.

Along the way all sorts of usages and institutions are criticized: criminal laws and their method of enforcement; the use of informers and torture; and punishment for witchcraft and sorcery. Slavery is attacked, and intolerance. Indeed, hardly any aspect of government is neglected.

Its brilliant generalizations are scattered among endless digressions containing observations from ancient and modern history, contemporary gossip, travellers' tales, and spicy anecdotes. At times, one feels that Montesquieu had not mastered his materials, but they had mastered him. Later Philosophes failed usually to see his intentions, and incorporated undigested bits from the work into their own writings. Voltaire tried to discredit the book and criticized isolated passages, as did Helvétius and some other Philosophes. But the work was widely read in France and all over Europe. It was both lavishly praised and severely criticized. Montesquieu wrote a short but brilliant *Defence* of the book. The Sorbonne tried in vain to get it censored, and the Papacy put it on the *Index*, both of which moves increased its circulation.

Within two years after its publication the book was circulating in an English translation. In this form it became well-known to Franklin, Adams, Madison, Hamilton, and Jefferson. *The Spirit of the Laws* became a veritable classic in the English colonies in America, and in the young United States. Its emphasis on the separation of powers was embodied in the *American Constitution* of 1787. *The Spirit of the Laws* was very influential in the formation of the French *Constitution of 1791*, in the *Charter of 1814*, in Napoleon's *Acte Additionnel*, in the *Spanish Constitution of 1812*, in the constitutions of 1820 of Piedmont and Naples, in the *Belgian Constitution of 1831*, and in a number of other constitutions, especially in Latin America.

Montesquieu was the founder of the comparative method in politics, and the whole study of historical jurisprudence dates from *The Spirit of the Laws*. He made law and government a concrete study based on the examination of facts. Moreover he made the discovery that whole groups of facts were essential to the understanding of both law and government. All in all, though *The Spirit of the Laws* is more conservative than revolutionary it was one of the most influential books of the French Enlightenment. *The Spirit of the Laws* is a work of great originality, and it is an important milestone in the development of modern political science and sociology.

4

VOLTAIRE

The great luminary of the Enlightenment not only in France but in all Europe was Voltaire (1694-1778). Born and educated under Louis XIV, he lived and wrote almost to the eve of the French Revolution. "To name Voltaire," wrote Victor Hugo, "is to characterize the entire Eighteenth Century." "Italy had a Renaissance and Germany had a Reformation, but France had Voltaire," writes one critic. "He was for his country both Renaissance and Reformation, and half the Revolution. He carried on the skepticism of Montaigne and earthy humor of Rabelais. He fought superstition and corruption more savagely and effectively than Luther or Erasmus, Calvin, Knox, or Melanchthon; he helped to make the powder with which Mirabeau and Marat, Danton, and Robespierre blew up the Old Regime."

1. Early Life and Interests

Voltaire, whose family name was Arouet, was born in Paris of a well-to-do, middle class family. He was educated by the Jesuits who formed his taste along classical lines. He studied law for a time, began to write plays and to circulate in the salons of Paris where he attracted attention because of his wit.

He wrote a clever poem satirizing the Regent, the Duke of Orleans, and spent eleven months in prison for his pains. By twenty-four, he was famous as a playwright. Next, forced to leave Paris by fear of arrest, he spent some time in Holland where he was impressed by the religious toleration that prevailed there, and by the freedom of the press. Voltaire then returned to Paris, got into a quarrel with a nobleman who had him beaten by hired thugs and then imprisoned for two weeks. On leaving prison on condition he would leave the country, Voltaire betook himself to England where he spent three years.

This sojourn in England was a turning point in his young life. While there, he found his reputation as a playwright had preceded him, and he met Swift, Pope, Bolingbroke, and Congreve, and, with a letter to the French ambassador in London, was received in literary and social circles. In England Voltaire learned to speak and write English well. Endlessly energetic and curious, Voltaire looked into many aspects of English life which he inevitably compared with life as he knew it in France. The first result of Voltaire's English sojourn was his *Philosophic Letters on the English* of 1733. Here, he popularized the ideas of Bacon, Locke, Newton, and a number of English thinkers, including some deists. He showed great admiration for the religious freedom and toleration in England, and the freedom of the press. Voltaire tells about Newton's funeral, which he attended, and which showed a great nation honoring a scientist as a national hero. This leads him to praise the high regard paid to men of letters and scientists in England. Voltaire praised the sincerity and simplicity of the Quakers, and he described other Protestant sects. This leads him to the idea that religious ceremonies count for little, and that conduct is of first importance. "An Englishman goes to heaven," he declared, "by the road which pleases him." Diversity of belief and a lively discussion of the nature of God and religion did not prevent economic prosperity or lead to a decline of morals. Much attention is given to English parliamentary usages, part of the account based on Voltaire's visits to the House of Commons. He then points out that taxes are fairly distributed in England, and that—unlike in France—both nobles and clerics must pay taxes. "The peasant," he declares, "does not have his feet pinched by wooden shoes; he eats white bread; he is well dressed, he is not afraid to increase the number of his cattle or to cover his roof with tile for fear that his taxes be raised next year."

Voltaire praises the respect given in England to businessmen, and points out that the nobles perform useful services to the state. England is a land that arrests men only on a warrant and gives him an early trial by jury. He even includes Shakespeare whom he characterized as "a barbarian of genius who did not follow the neoclassical unities of time, place, and action." All in all much of English civilization was covered. There is no doubt that Voltaire idealized the English way of life. Only a portion of the English population enjoyed the advantages he described. Liberty of person was not secure from the press-gang; political comment was at times sharply limited; Quakers, Unitarians, and Catholics suffered civil disabilities; the law was antiquated, cruel, and tangled up in complexities, and often administered in the interests of the rich against the poor. Parliament was unreformed, and did not represent the English people.

These *Letters* were Voltaire's first masterpiece in prose, and the work made an enormous impression both in France and in Europe. Rousseau declared that these *Letters* had taught him to think. By indirection, Voltaire had criticized many things in France: oppressive religious unity, the wealth of the clergy, royal absolutism, the privileges of the French nobility, and the lack of freedom of thought. The *Letters* were a bombshell dropped on the Old Regime in France. Their style, which was to be typical of Voltaire's later writing, was one of short crisp sentences full of biting irony and wit and very incisive and easy to read. The state censor refused the right to publish the book, and it was published anonymously and secretly in Rouen; Voltaire's arrest was ordered, and the book was officially burned. But it still continued to circulate, and Voltaire was given credit for writing it. He had gone to England as a poet and a wit, and he returned a Philosophe.

Wanted by the police, Voltaire then went into semi-hiding on the estate of his mistress, Mme. de Châtelet, and he lived with her at Cirey in Lorraine from 1733 to 1749. Mme. de Châtelet was a lady of enormous learning, and Voltaire's years at Cirey were rich in intellectual experience. She turned Voltaire's attention to science, especially physics and chemistry, to metaphysics, for which however he never acquired a taste, to moral philosophy, and to the writing of history. During this period, in spite of the government's condemnation of his writing, Voltaire was elected to the French Academy, and even served a while as an official of the court of Louis XV. Here he offended Mme. de Pompadour, and had to leave, still a very controversial figure. Voltaire soon received an invitation to visit the Court of Frederick the Great of Prussia. Here in Berlin he received a warm welcome, but as in France, found his position as a courtier irksome. Following bitter recriminations on both sides, over very minor issues, Voltaire left Berlin, and, after two years of wandering over Europe, bought an estate near Geneva. He finally settled at Ferney where part of his holdings were in France, part in Switzerland, and part in the semi-independent state of Geneva. Here he could defy the police.

Voltaire was by this time a well-to-do man. His writings were bringing in a good income, and he had in addition inherited money from his father, and gained wealth by financial speculation. He was always a shrewd, and sometimes a stingy businessman. When Voltaire settled at Ferney, he was still known chiefly as the writer of a number of successful neoclassical plays in the style of Corneille and Racine and as the author of a body of poetry. Chief among his longer poems was the *Henriade*, an epic on the life and rule of Henry IV. The poem praised Henry IV as an able and effective ruler and as a great advocate of religious toleration. Always a prolific writer, Voltaire had continued to publish while he was living with the brilliant and stimulating Mme. de Châtelet, and, after her death, at the court of Frederick the Great.

2. Voltaire at Ferney

At Ferney where he spent the last twenty some years of his life, he lived like a great lord entertaining visitors from all over Europe. Voltaire was now very wealthy. He had a magnificent establishment with a model farm, a watch and clock making factory, a church which he had built and where Voltaire went to pray to his deistic God, a private theater, a magnificent library, and a staff of sixty persons. There was something new every day, and never the same thing two days in a row. He poured forth a seemingly endless stream of literary work: pamphlets and tracts, novels, short stories, plays, satires, histories, and letters. Everywhere he attacked abuses in religion, law, and politics wherever and whenever he encountered them. He was too impatient and hot-footed a writer to achieve a supreme masterpiece in any field. He wrote scarcely a page that was not a criticism of some abuse or a recommendation for some reform. Voltaire commanded a brilliant style unsurpassed in its irony and audacity, and he was read everywhere as no man before him in European letters. "As a popularizer," said Taine, "he had no rival."

One preoccupation that ran through much of Voltaire's life was his interest in history. From history, he drew much of the material for his plays and tales, and, as early as the time he was composing the *Philosophic Letters on the English,* he wrote a *Life of Charles XII* of Sweden. Here he took his subject from nearly contemporary events, and he produced a brilliant work of absorbing interest about one of the strangest characters of the time. In form, however, it was a conventional biography mostly about politics, diplomacy, and war. It showed accurate documentation and impartial treatment, and an interest in men who knew about the events of Charles XII's career. So far as it was propaganda the book showed the folly of conquests. "If any princes or ministers should find disagreeable truths in this work," he wrote "let them remember that, being public men, they are accountable to the public for their actions; that this is the price they pay for their grandeur; that history is a witness and not a flatterer, and that the only way to oblige men to speak well of us is to do good." Charles XII's life "should teach kings how much a pacific and happy government is superior to military glory." Voltaire's historical writing from the beginning showed that he had a sharp eye to select the picturesque and to use telling details to present a picture or a situation that impresses the reader by its vividness and its coherence.

During the years Voltaire lived with the gifted Mme. de Châtelet they had often discussed the writing of history. Mme. de Châtelet complained that she found in modern histories only a record of events without connection or sequence, an account of battles which settled nothing, a study which overwhelmed the mind without illuminating it. Voltaire also had read in Francis Bacon's *Advancement of Learning* the need for a history of learning and culture, and in Fénelon the need for a history of social phenomena.

So while he was at the court of Frederick the Great at Potsdam, Voltaire undertook to finish a history of the *Age of Louis XIV*. Here he produced a general cultural history that subordinated wars and statecraft to the story of a whole civilization. The account of the reign of Louis XIV included a description of the central government in war and peace, many chapters on what is now called social history, and four chapters on literature, science, and art. In a letter he explained his methods, "the enlightened spirit now prevalent among the leading nations of Europe requires us to go to the bottom of history, instead of skimming its surface, as other writers have done. People now wish to know how a nation grew, the changes of its population, the difference in the number of soldiers at different times, the nature and growth of its commerce, what acts have sprung up within the country and what have been introduced from elsewhere and perfected there, the changes in the average revenue of the state, the birth and expansion of its navy, and the relative number of its nobles, clergy, and cultivators of the soil." Voltaire's purpose was to rescue history from the dead hand of the antiquary and to make it useful and didactic.

No previous historian could compare with Voltaire in the width of his views, or in real originality of treatment. Here Voltaire made himself the father of modern cultural history, and began a great revolution in historical writing. His *Louis XIV* was his first profoundly original creation. In the opening sentence, Voltaire declared his purpose, "It is not only the life of Louis XIV I propose to write but a much greater thing. I shall try to paint for posterity not the actions of one man, but the spirit of the men of the most enlightened age of all time." He set aside the old analytic method that adhered to chronology, and adopted a topical method of treatment. The coverage was superbly catholic and included not only the story of Louis XIV's actions in war and peace, but also tales about court life, descriptions of the government of France with facts about its laws, administration, commerce, and a full description of its cultural achievements. "A lock on a canal joining two seas," he wrote, "a picture by Poussin, a good tragedy, the discovery of a truth, are things a thousand times more precious than all the narratives of campaigns." Everywhere, he regarded history as the clash of ideas operating through individuals, classes, and institutions—to that extent Voltaire did have a sort of philosophy of history. Voltaire was reasonably objective, but did not fail to give praise and blame. He had consulted many men who had lived in the age of Louis XIV, read both published and unpublished memoirs, and, in some cases, had even consulted archives. Voltaire actually worked at the book for nearly twenty years.

Diderot declared of the work, pointing out its Liberal biases, "Other historians relate facts to inform us of facts. You relate them in order to arouse in our hearts a profound hatred of lying, superstition, fanaticism, and tyranny, and thus anger remains after the memory of facts had disappeared." Even in writing history, Voltaire was writing propaganda.

Continuing his interest in history, Voltaire at Ferney produced his most remarkable historical work, his *Essay on Manners*. This related the story of mankind, in both West and East, from the time of Charlemagne to that of Louis XIV. "I wish," he wrote, "to write a history not of wars, but of society, and ascertain how men lived, and what were the arts which they cultivated. My object is the history of the human mind, and not a mere detailing of many facts; nor am I concerned with the history of great lords, but I want to know what were the steps by which men passed from barbarism to civilization." The work has a magnificent sweep, but it also contains a lot of humanitarian proselytizing; it is severe on kings who only loved military glory, and on the weaknesses of the Church. Voltaire shows that the general progress of culture is incompatible with political oppression and religious intolerance. Montesquieu judged Voltaire harshly as an historian. "Voltaire," he wrote, "is like the monks who write not for the subject they are treating, but for the glory of the order. Voltaire is writing for his monastery." (But frankly Montesquieu had sometimes done the same.)

The *Essay on Manners*, like the *Age of Louis XIV*, is marred by too much propaganda, by a lack of understanding of the Middle Ages and the history of Christianity, by too hasty generalizations, and by many mistakes in facts. Voltaire, unlike Bossuet who believed in providence, had no elaborate philosophy of history; Voltaire believed that chance is the governing factor in human affairs, and that the presence or absence of great men in history is a very important factor in determining the history of a period. Man determined his own destiny, and men could change. Voltaire did, in spite of the folly and weakness of mankind, see some progress in history through the spread of enlightenment. The *Age of Louis XIV* which he followed by an *Age of Louis XV*, and the *Essay on*

Manners created a new type of cultural history, which was one of the most original inventions of the Age of Enlightenment in France.

Parallel with Voltaire's life-long interest in history went an interest in politics. He did not, however, produce anything in political thought as original as his best historical writing. In Voltaire's time, there were in France three main currents of Liberal political thought. The first was the idea of a thoroughly enlightened despotism, of which the Prussia of Frederick the Great was a fair example. To this ideal most of the Philosophes, including Voltaire, adhered. Second was the idea of a limited monarchy as it existed in England, the type of monarchy praised by Locke and Montesquieu. And third there was democracy as expounded by Rousseau. Both the last two types of government, in somewhat perverted forms, were tried in the French Revolution.

Voltaire, like many of the Philosophes, believed in man provided he were educated and used his reason. But the average run of men were illiterate, unreasonable, and superstitious, and needed the guidance of an enlightened ruler. "It must please the animals," he said, "when they see how foolishly men behave." "The populace," Voltaire declared, "are oxen who need a yoke, a goad, and hay." As for him, he preferred, he said, "to obey a fine lion much stronger than himself to two hundred rats of his own species!" But there were severe limitations on enlightened despotism. The enlightened despot must obey the laws and be sure that they were fairly enforced for all classes. Also the monarch must foster education and the arts and sciences, allow trial by jury, complete religious toleration, freedom of speech and the press, commercial liberty, and respect for private property. Above all, the enlightened monarch must avoid the capricious and unpredictable imposition of his own whims. These Philosophes found the monarchy of Louis XV lacking in nearly every aspect of good government. His government did not act under law; many of the laws were bad; the government spent too much money on wars and royal extravagance; the system of taxation was unfair, and the Church needed curbing.

Voltaire believed that tradition did justify government differences in different places. He was extremely flexible; constitutional and representative governments are good for some countries, as for example England. But for France, constitutional government would simply keep feudal anarchy alive, and would allow the Church to perpetuate all its abuses. Voltaire even had some sympathy with republicanism as a natural, free, humane, and peaceful form of political association, but practical conditions, especially the ignorance of the masses, made it an impossible form of government for France. Voltaire was not the man to offer a blueprint for a Utopia. He was always a practical and hard-headed realist.

Voltaire was particularly attached to the idea of toleration and a free press. At Ferney, he conducted campaigns against the abuses of the courts in the matter of justice and toleration. The most famous case, about which he got the whole of Europe talking, involved a miserable piece of intolerance and injustice. A Protestant in Toulouse, one Calas, had been condemned and tortured, so that he died soon afterward, on the charge of having murdered his son to prevent the son's conversion to Catholicism. Voltaire took up the case, and so aroused public opinion that Calas, though dead, was retried and exonerated. It was proved that the son had committed suicide and the government paid an indemnity to Calas' family. Calas was proved completely innocent. Several similar cases were given a great airing by Voltaire. In few ways did Voltaire so clearly show the power of his pen. In 1763, Voltaire published his *Treatise on Toleration*, an eloquent appeal for religious freedom, which shows that liberation causes no trouble in England and Holland, and that governments should remember that all men are brothers under God. In his *Philosophic Dictionary*, a brilliant work of propaganda for his ideas, Voltaire wrote, "What is tolerance? It is a privilege to which human nature is entitled. We are all so compounded of weakness and error that it behooves us mutually to forgive one another's follies. This is the first law of nature. Every man persecuting another for not being of his own opinions is a monster."

In his later years, Voltaire became more serious and fought more savagely; he was always using the expression "Crush the infamous thing." Though this was particularly directed against the organized churches, it really meant to crush anywhere the use of arbitrary, entrenched, and senseless power by an absolute Church or state.

No interest that Voltaire had lasted longer in his life—from beginning to end—than his interest in religion, though again he never managed to say anything very original on the subject. Like some of the other Philosophes, Voltaire believed in a natural religion that included the belief in God and in a world of future rewards and punishments. This natural religion was believed—and wrongly—to prevail among all peoples. Natural religion was engraved on the hearts of men everywhere. It was as old as creation, and embraced as heroes men like Confucius, Socrates, and Cicero. All this natural religion was opposed to organized Christianity with its miracles, its supernatural doctrines, and its positive religious duties. Natural religion, however, had been corrupted by the machinations of rulers and priests.

If he attacked existing religious practices in Europe and elsewhere, Voltaire remained a convinced deist. "If God did not exist," he declared, "we would have to invent him to explain the universe." His proofs of the existence of God were first, that there was an orderly system of the universe, second, creation requires a first cause, a prime mover, and, finally, good and evil must have a final sanction. Voltaire feared atheism as likely to bring discredit on the Philosophes, and as a threat to social stability among the masses.

Voltaire's criticism of religious beliefs and practices reached its height in the exaggerated attacks he made on the Bible and on the historic churches. He attacked the contradictions in the Bible and the improbabilities of miracles. He used endless irony and wit against what he regarded as the childish absurdities in the Bible and in the teachings of the churches. The greatest vials of his wrath were reserved for his attack on the Old Testament. Voltaire doubts the existence of Moses, calls the Pentateuch absurd and barbarous, brands the Jews as a "horde of Asiatic bandits" and holds up their history as a "collection of fables, equally outraging good sense, virtue, nature, and the Deity." As to the New Testament he calls Jesus "a good fellow, a coarse peasant, and a fanatic like George Fox" (founder of the Quakers). In all that he wrote about religion, Voltaire is in no way original except in his exaggerations. Nearly all of his religious ideas came from English and Continental deists, and from critics like Bayle. But he was read by many more people than had read his precursors or his contemporaries.

To readers of the Twentieth Century, Voltaire's diatribes against lawless and absolute monarchy, and a persecuting Church have lost most of their point. Both his type of deism and his attacks on organized religion seem very dated. Also his poetry, including his epic the *Henriade* and a mock epic on Joan of Arc called the *Maid*, now seem flat, insipid, and jejune. But many of his tales are as alive today as when they were written. Among these tales the most outstanding one is a short, picaresque novel, *Candide*, perhaps Voltaire's one literary masterpiece. It was published anonymously as were most of his works, but everyone knew there was only one man who could have written it. No book in a comparable number of pages contains so much devastating wit. It is perhaps the world's masterpiece of skepticism, but behind it lies a genuine moral earnestness. *Candide* is the story of the adventures of a naive young man in Europe and South America. Through the tale runs a criticism and a satirizing of the idea of Leibniz and

Pope that this is "the best of all possible worlds." After all sorts of escapades, including the experiencing of the Lisbon earthquake, he finally settles down to "cultivate his own garden" as Voltaire says. By this he means that men must recognize reality and live with it, and be satisfied working with one's own task. All can agree on the value of productive work, as one character in *Candide* says, "work saves us from three great evils: boredom, vice, and want."

Voltaire's character was the strangest mixture of contradictions. He could be petty, spiteful, and vindictive, and, then next very generous and understanding with others. He was vain, flippant, obscene, impulsive, and on a few occasions dishonest when it suited his line of argument. Yet he was often lavish of his energy and purse in helping others, able to kill with the stroke of his pen, and yet disarmed at the first gesture of reconciliation. He was very jealous of the reputation of Montesquieu, and somewhat jealous of the repute of Rousseau. And Voltaire was always something of a snob. At one party where he was present he remarked, "I think we are all princes or poets." Few have surpassed him in the range of his interests, his energy, and the wealth of information he possessed about the world and the life of man. But his mind was discursive rather than orderly or concentrated, and he failed to construct a systematic account of the infinite number of subjects he treated.

Voltaire lacked patience, as he lacked concentration, and he moved always by jerks. He was always a practical moralist with a passionate and never flagging desire to reform everything according to the dictates of reason and common sense. His utterances palpitate with life, but always bear the mark of haste. Voltaire was essentially a crusader like Luther, always stronger in destruction than in positive construction. He was, says one historian, "the Spirit of the Enlightenment incarnate with all its virtues and all its faults. Everything he said and wrote was as stimulating as the coffee on which he lived." "His conversation" wrote Boswell, "is the most brilliant I ever heard. I said to myself he is either Erasmus or the Devil." No man ever did more to kill superstition and hocus-pocus. Heine declared that "in the great war for the liberation of humanity, Voltaire's name will always stand first." "If we judge men by what they have done," said Lamartine, "then Voltaire is un-contestably the greatest writer of modern Europe."

5

DIDEROT

1. His Life and Work

Denis Diderot (1713-1784) was the most versatile of the Philosophes. He wrote on philosophy, science, technology, theology, and education, and he also wrote plays, novels, essays, and art and dramatic criticism. He was the typical Philosophe who rejected all authority and tradition that interfered with free inquiry and violated the natural rights of man. He believed that religious intolerance was the greatest enemy of progress, and he pleaded passionately for toleration and intellectual freedom. Sainte-Beuve called Diderot "the Spokesman of the Century."

Diderot's life was a hard one, an affair of ups and downs. When he was in his early years as a writer, he was sometimes on the verge of starvation, and though he became a famous author and was an indefatigable worker, he never had more than a modest income, and he was never elected to the French Academy. Also he spent a term in prison. If on the one hand, he sometimes did not know where his next meal was coming from, on the other, he was later for a time a favorite at the court of Catharine the Great of Russia. Diderot's head was always full of all sorts of ideas, plans, projects, and dreams.

Never was there a richer or more receptive personality. He was so all-embracing in his outlook that he always kept a soft spot in his heart for ideas that his reason told him to abandon. Though an atheist, he, at times, praised the Catholic religion. So there were various Diderots within a single body.

Diderot was born in Eastern France, in Champagne, at Langres. His father was a skilled craftsman, a cutler, who had invented a number of surgical instruments. For over two hundred years, the family had been in the cutlery craft at Langres. Diderot's father was a good, solid, bourgeois who did not understand his son, and often quarreled with him. His father was much respected in Langres by his neighbors and friends, but he had no experience that enabled him to understand his gifted son. Diderot, though he did not always get on with his father, greatly respected him, and twice made him the central character of an important literary work. The father wrote to the young Diderot, "My son, an excellent pillow is that of reason, but I find that my head rests even more softly on that of religion and the laws." The father eventually learned to accept his rebellious son with good-humored tolerance.

The young Diderot was educated by the Jesuits in whose school at Langres he won many prizes. Then his father took him to Paris for further training. His father hoped he would enter the Church, and, failing that, would study law. After leaving the secondary school in Paris, Diderot studied a while at the University of Paris. After Diderot left school, he read law for a time, but found he was not interested. Then he tried tutoring wealthy youths, but he hated that. And finally he found work as a free-lance author taking such miserably paid positions as he could find. Circumstances were already stamping the youthful Diderot with nervous irritability and a changeable disposition that was to characterize his later life. All the while Diderot was devoting all the time he could get to reading and study. The range of his interests in Greek, Latin, French, Italian, and English was wide, and he was an omnivorous reader. He loved the exciting life of Paris, and took one mistress after another. Later, he composed an *Essay on Women* which showed him a keen observer of feminine psychology.

At the age of thirty, Diderot married, but, though he had four children, only one of whom, a favorite daughter, survived, the marriage was unhappy. His wife was uneducated and incapable of understanding her husband. But no matter whom Diderot would have married, he was too inconstant and too much the libertine to make a faithful husband. Later he met a remarkable and gifted young woman, Sophie Volland, who became for years his mistress and his inspiration. As a free-lance writer, Diderot translated from English a history of Greece, an essay of Shaftesbury, and a medical dictionary. About this time, he met the young Rousseau, and they became close friends sharing many of the same ideas and interests for the next fifteen years. Both were fascinated with new ideas, both were ill-at-ease with strangers and in formal society, and both had a self-conscious independence. Diderot also became a good friend of Condillac.

In his introduction to an essay by Shaftesbury, Diderot declared that human nature is naturally good, and that men need only to be shown where their best course lies. Their reason will carry them to right action, and passion and egoism will be set aside. Later Diderot wrote "Nature has not made us vicious; it is bad education, bad examples, and bad legislation that have corrupted us." He believed that the recompense of virtue lies in itself, in the happiness it will furnish. The punishment of vice is in itself and is inevitable. Men are possessed of an innate sympathy for their fellow creatures, and this sympathy enables men to overcome their selfish egoism. These ideas he shared with Rousseau. Also in his introduction to Shaftesbury's essay, Diderot declares that religion and virtue are separate, and virtue is the more important. The spectacle of virtue, he writes, "inflames me with ardor and enthusiasm; then it seems my heart expands within me, that it swims; an indefinable sensation traverses me, I can scarcely breathe, and my eyes are filled with tears." The sensibility and emotionality shown here came partly from Diderot's nature, and partly from Rousseau and, finally, from reading Richardson and a number of other English writers. Here we see Diderot as the forerunner of a Romantic generation.

In an early work, *Essay on Merit and Virtue*, Diderot states that he is a Christian, but he evidently means by this that he believes in the ethical teachings of Jesus rather than an allegiance to the Church. At this time, Diderot was a deist who believed in the immortality of the soul and the concept of a world of future rewards and punishments. Morality is founded on man's social and natural requirements, and not on church-

made rules. In his next work, *Philosophic Thoughts*, Diderot
moves further away from Christianity, and condemns the un-
reasonableness of organized Christianity. He cast doubt on the
authenticity of the Scriptures, and the truth of miracles, he is
here rigidly rationalistic. "Skepticism," he declares, "is the
first step toward truth." There is little that is original here with
Diderot; it had been said earlier by English deists and French
writers like Voltaire. It does show Diderot on the road from
deism to atheism. He is still unable to make up his mind.
Truth for him was always complex, and he is, by nature, less
dogmatic than many of the other Philosophes.

Another interesting aspect of the *Philosophic Thoughts* is
Diderot's defense of the passions as furnishing energy for all
activities, and inspiration in the arts. Without men's passions
reason would be arid and fruitless. The *Philosophic Thoughts*
was Diderot's first literary success. This was due less to its
originality than to the enthusiastic and highly personal style
in which the book was written. The work was published
anonymously with the Hague on the title page. The Parlement of Paris condemned the book to be burned by the public
hangman. It took a little time before the authorship was
known, but its contents and its condemnation by the public
authorities gave it an extensive circulation. Another similar
work, *Skeptic's Walk*, was seized in manuscript, by the police,
and was never published till 1830. Though written in a lively
style that was bound to attract attention, these early writings
of Diderot are not very original. They seem to be a combina-
tion of what are usually regarded as the ideas of Voltaire with

those of the younger Rousseau. Diderot, however, did not necessarily derive all of his ideas from either; some of them may have come out of the currents of thought that were becoming common at the time.

Diderot loved to write, and he next tried his hand at a light and licentious novel, *The Indiscreet Jewels.* The book contains thrusts at women, the soul, the clergy, magistrates, the court, academicians, and pedants. But he defends the King's favorite, Mme. de Pompadour, as a friend of enlightenment. Most remarkable is Diderot's attack on the classical French theater. He exalts realism and condemns convention. Corneille and Racine, instead of imitating nature, copy the ancients. The classical rule of the three unities deprives their work of probability. This was Diderot's first important venture in literary criticism. The work was published in 1748, and soon went through three editions. It was followed by another spicy tale, *The White Bird*, though this was never published till after his death. At the same time, Diderot did publish five *Memoirs* on mathematical and scientific subjects.

Diderot had, by this time, come to be occupied with the editing of the *Encyclopedia*, but he still found time to do other work. The editing of a huge, general *Encyclopedia* that would cover nearly all subjects became Diderot's chief task for the next twenty years. His next important book to attract wide attention was his *Letter on the Blind for the Use of Those Who See.* Diderot's chief concern is the origin and validity of man's moral ideas and of his idea of God. He believed both were derived from social experience. Diderot was the first to understand well the psychology of the blind, and to point out how one sense is substituted for another. He proposed a system of educating the blind by a system of touch symbols. Amidst solid psychological observation, Diderot for the first time states his atheism. The work contains in embryo a theory of organic evolution in nature on which, however, Diderot does not elaborate. The book was widely read and commented upon, and the originality of Diderot's discussion was greatly admired and brought him the friendship of Voltaire. Diderot had by this time become an atheist, though he never explains exactly why. It was the author's atheism that aroused the government authorities, and Diderot was obliged to spend three and a half months in prison at Vincennes.

Two years after the *Letter on the Blind* Diderot published a somewhat similar *Letter on the Deaf and Dumb for the Use of Those who Hear and Speak.* Here he is particularly interested in the origin and growth of languages. The work is very original, and contains some sound psychological observations on the use by men of hearing and speaking. The author points out that words do not merely convey ideas; they have the power of creating reactions and associations so that the total effect of a word far surpasses its literal meaning. Poetry, for example, is far more than a mere conveyance of thought, more even than harmony and rhythm. In both the work on the blind and deaf-mutes, Diderot's thoughts are new; he is one of the founders of modern psychology. This time, in the work on deaf-mutes, he carefully avoids any mention of his atheistic ideas.

In about 1750, Diderot became well acquainted with Grimm, son of a German Lutheran pastor, who had settled in Paris as a tutor, and was the author of an occasional circular letter sent to subscribers, with some of the latest news of Paris and France. To the same circle belonged Rousseau and Helvétius. Grimm and Diderot became firm friends. Their temperaments were in great contrast. Grimm was clever but unemotional and self-possessed, whereas one writer says Diderot was "a volcano in permanent eruption." Both men were deeply interested in music, the theater, in ethical analyses, and literary criticism. Although Grimm was ten years younger than Diderot, he had a great influence on him. "Grimm," says Sainte-Beuve, "becoming the most French of the Germans, was attracted, by a sort of natural affinity, to Diderot, the most German of Frenchmen."

By this time, Diderot's fame was spreading beyond France, and in 1751 he was elected to the Berlin Academy which, under the sponsorship of Frederick the Great, was becoming a mecca for persecuted French authors. Voltaire at the time was living at the court of Frederick the Great. The same year the first volume of the *Encyclopedia* appeared under Diderot's editorship. The volume attracted the attention of Holbach who soon became a close friend of Diderot. Holbach was a wealthy German nobleman who preferred to live in Paris where he entertained lavishly, and gave financial aid to the Philosophes. Among Holbach's close friends, besides Diderot, were Grimm, d'Alembert, Turgot, Buffon, Helvétius, Condillac, and, for a time, Rousseau. No salon in Paris attracted so many leaders of the Liberal party as did that of Holbach. Diderot soon came to be Holbach's favorite; they were both atheists.

When the second volume of the *Encyclopedia* appeared, it caused a great uproar, and the government ordered both volumes one and two suppressed, and forbade the printing of further volumes. The order read, in part, "His majesty has recognized that in these two volumes they have presumed to insert several maxims tending to destroy royal authority, to establish the spirit of independence and revolt, and, beneath obscure and equivocal terms, to raise the foundations of error, moral corruption, irreligion, and incredulity." The government censors had first approved of the two volumes, but, before they had gone to press, numerous insertions had been made. Diderot's papers were seized by the police and turned over to the Jesuits, but the Jesuits were unable to make head or tail out of Diderot's notes, and the notes were later returned to the author. But the government censor, who was sympathetic to the *Encyclopedia*, secretly told Diderot to go ahead.

Diderot, in the meanwhile, became involved in a quarrel as to which was better, the Italian or the French style of opera writing. The Philosophes favored the Italian style as less stilted and artificial than the French style. The Philosophes made great fun of the shepherds and shepherdesses, the mythical gods, and the inane ballets of the French opera. Music for a time monopolized talk in the salons. The partisans of the Italian style were fighting for simplicity and naturalness. Diderot called for a closer accord between music and libretto, and insisted that music must communicate ideas and emotions as well as merely please. Actually both Italian and French styles of opera were rather vapid and inane; especially were the librettos weak. As Voltaire said, "What is too silly to be said, is sung." But in 1754, Italian opera was banned and the lively quarrel, for the time being, was over. The dispute, in which Diderot took a prominent part, shows how deep were his esthetic interests.

The third and fourth volumes of the *Encyclopedia* now appeared, and went unchallenged. The interference of the censorship and the frequent literary and artistic quarrels in which Diderot was involved, made him very moody and, at times, extremely pessimistic. His ups and downs also gave Diderot frequent attacks of indigestion. His old gaiety and light-heartedness slowly disappeared. He declared he envied obscure writers who have neither worries nor fame. But Diderot's fundamental energy and optimism would again come to the surface, though any annoyance or difficulty would upset him. By this time, Diderot had become reconciled with his father. Diderot's wife had visited in Langres, and had been well received, and, after eleven years, Diderot himself went to visit his father. The old cutler was now proud of his son's literary eminence, and preferred Diderot to his brother who was a somewhat dour priest. "I have two sons," declared the father, "one will surely be a saint, and I fear that the other will be damned, but I cannot live with the saint, and I am happy with the sinner."

Diderot, although always busy with the editing of the *En-*

cyclopedia, found occasion to write other works. His deep interest in science appeared in a work of 1753, the *Thoughts on the Interpretation of Nature*. Here his long concern with chemistry, zoology, physiology, and medicine takes on a materialistic tone in which Diderot prepared the way for Nineteenth Century materialism. He declared, "we are on the threshold of a great revolution in the sciences." The only road to scientific progress is that of experimentation, and a patient collection of facts. But insight and imagination must be used in interpreting facts. The work contains a remarkable foreshadowing of the atomic nature of matter, and again of the idea of organic evolution. The work later was greatly admired by Auguste Comte, the father of Positivism, who said of Diderot that "he was the greatest genius of the Eighteenth Century."

In 1757, Diderot finally broke with Rousseau. Diderot had become disgusted with Rousseau's antisocial attitudes, and his primitivism; also Diderot became estranged because of Rousseau's deism. There was in addition a quarrel over the friendship of a woman. The break was more the fault of Rousseau who was, by nature, more difficult than Diderot, and was always inclined to isolate himself from all men. Rousseau became the enemy of all the Philosophes, and joined the chorus of criticism of them, though always criticizing from his own peculiar point of view. He attacked the idea that the world was a machine, rejected society as it then existed, scientific progress, and rational enlightenment as the other Philosophes conceived it. The wonder is that the friendship of Diderot and

Rousseau lasted as long as it did. The current of thought represented by Diderot was, in part, one leading to a scientific and rationalist mentality; that held by Rousseau led to Romanticism and anti-rational movements.

In the meantime, the indefatigable Diderot was editing volume after volume of the *Encyclopedia,* and turning out pamphlets, books of both tales and plays, as well as art and literary criticism. In 1759, the government ordered the publication of the *Encyclopedia* stopped and forbade the selling of any more copies of the volumes already issued. It looked to Diderot as if "the great work of his life," as he called it, was never going to be finished. He took the attitude, however, of waiting to see if things would not take a better turn.

Fortunately, Diderot had other interests. For the theater, he wrote several plays, and published some critical essays on the dramatic art. When he was writing, most plays were still written in the traditional neoclassic style. But a few writers, including Diderot, had begun to treat in a realistic manner, the lives of persons in the middle and lower classes. These plays, written in prose, usually inculcated a moral lesson, and were written with a good deal of sentimentality. The settings were contemporary. In 1757 Diderot had published his first play, *The Natural Son.* It showed, as did his novels, the influence of Richardson and other English writers. Later Diderot wrote an essay *In Praise of Richardson.* The next year, he published a second play, *The Father of the Family,* and several essays on the dramatic art. His idea in writing the plays and the essays was to show that a new kind of drama was demanded by the public, one that dealt with everyday problems of the middle class. Diderot declared that the theater could teach morals better than the Church. He believed that settings should be realistic as should also be the acting. He attacked stilted and artificial conventions in the acting of his day, and wanted the setting and acting of plays to be a direct reflection of life itself. Diderot appreciated Shakespeare as Voltaire did not. He was also one of the first writers to see the social function of literature whose object was the criticism of life. Diderot's plays and his writings on the drama were widely read, but the plays were not successful on the stage. The author was too subjective to produce living characters. The plays were full of passionate and highly emotional ranting and copious tears. Diderot believed that the language of the heart is more varied and deeper than reason. Here he shows clearly the growth of sentimentalism and emotionality in the Eighteenth Century. The plays, though failures on the stage, influenced other dramatists including Lessing in Germany.

Diderot's novels, though better than his plays, showed the same weakness, i.e., an inability to write dialogue that seems deeply related to the people who speak it. One of his better tales was *The Nun*, a penetrating study of what the convent does to one unsuited for it. The character of *The Nun* is sympathetically portrayed. Against her personality is set that of three mothers superior with whom she had to deal. The first is kind and gentle and "dies in an agony of mystic despair"; the second is a woman of savage cruelty who behaves like a brute; and the third is a Lesbian who "expires amid the horrors of madness, remorse, and superstitious terror." Diderot's *The Nun* circulated in manuscript, but was not printed till 1796.

His most famous novel, *The Nephew of Rameau*, is concerned chiefly with the analysis of a completely alienated man who, at every point, is at war with society. As in *The Nun* the main character is brilliantly analyzed psychologically; one critic compares the hero with Hamlet, Faust, Richard III, and Don Quixote. *The Nephew of Rameau*, a minor masterpiece, was only published after Diderot's death. Diderot's literary tastes are definitely Romantic. He praised Ossian and Young's *Night Thoughts*; he appreciated, he said "something enormous, barbarian, savage," and he loved ruins and wild scenery. These tastes come out less in his novels and plays than in his essays and letters.

In the field of art criticism, Diderot was also an important innovator, and he may be said to have originated modern art criticism in France. In both literary and art criticism, Diderot emphasized the beauties rather than the faults of a work, and he always tried to put himself at the point of view of the subject and the creator of the work he was examining. His friend, Grimm, sent out, in manuscript, a bi-weekly newsletter to subscribers, mostly noblemen and rulers, in France and Germany. Grimm urged Diderot to write up current art exhibitions, the Salons, for his newsletter. Thus in 1759 Diderot wrote his first critical article on painting and sculpture. He gained information by talking to sculptors and painters, and watching them at work. His criticisms were very acute, and he helped to make esthetics a part of philosophy. In addition to these articles on art exhibitions, he wrote an article *On Beauty* for the *Encyclopedia*. Here he defined beauty as the perfect adaptation of the subject to its method of treatment. And he declared that the artist should create the illusion of truth rather than to copy nature exactly. This should be done by picking out the essential traits of the subject, and emphasizing them. Observation of nature and the careful selection of telling details should form the training of the artists, not copying from the ancients.

Diderot especially admired the paintings of Greuze and Chardin who chose subjects from the common people and treated them in a somewhat sentimental way. He especially liked Greuze's *The Village Bride*, of which he wrote "the subject is pathetic, and one feels overcome with secret emotion on looking at it." Diderot believed that art like literature should teach some moral lesson, and it could teach such lessons better than the Church. "I am not a Capuchin," he wrote, "yet I would hasten the coming of the day when painting and sculpture, more decent and moral, will think of contributing, together with the other arts, to inspire virtue and purify our manners." In spite of this, Diderot often enjoyed and praised lascivious pictures for their technical qualities. He usually began his criticism with a description of a painting or sculpture and then went on to set forth his own reactions to the work of art. No writer ever equalled Diderot's power to make the reader see for himself what the painter sought to achieve. His art criticism greatly influenced Delacroix and Baudelaire, and is still interesting reading today. Diderot liked a realistic portrayal of nature; he said he would give ten Watteaus for a single Teniers! Diderot's ideas and theories on art and literature are complex and disorganized, yet he was always concerned with the interpretation of beautiful nature, with conserving the truth of nature, and inspiring moral good in man.

In the meantime, Diderot and his publisher had decided to go on with the publishing of the *Encyclopedia*. It was to be done secretly, and no more volumes were to be put into circulation until the whole work was finished, and so the last ten volumes were all to be circulated at once. As Diderot wrote, "To abandon the work would be what the scoundrels who are persecuting us want us to do." Frederick the Great offered to have the whole enterprise moved to Berlin, and Catharine the Great made the same offer to transfer it all to St. Petersburg. But Diderot declined; he could not work so far away from his contributors. When the final volumes appeared, Diderot discovered that the publisher had cut out portions of some of the articles that he believed would give offense. This was a hard blow to Diderot, but now there was nothing he could do about it. At last, after twenty years of hard work the *Encyclopedia* was complete, except for some of the volumes of illustrations. The only reaction of the government was to send the publisher for a week to the Bastille.

Between 1763 and 1772, Diderot wrote *D'Alembert's Dream, The Paradox on Acting, The Nephew of Rameau, Jacques the Fatalist*, and a number of short stories. During this period, he became a more convinced atheist. In this period, Holbach's influence was paramount. "I would sacrifice my life," wrote Diderot, "if I could annihilate forever the notion of God." Religion with its superstitions, its hatreds, and its priests are all evil. Of all religions, Christianity was the worst, "the most absurd and the most atrocious in its dogma." Some of these ideas were elaborated in an imaginary dialogue which Diderot called *D'Alembert's Dream*. It was the most integrated system of materialism produced so far by the Philosophes. Here Diderot plunged into the controversies over the ultimate nature of matter and the meaning of life. He came close to explaining the cellular structure of living organisms and anticipated once again the theory of organic evolution. The work is full of keen observations on the origins of life and on the psychology of men and animals. His final materialistic conclusion, summed up in the *Salon of 1767*, was that "this world is only a mass of molecules. There is a law of necessity that works without design, without effort, without intelligence, and without progress." Much of Diderot's thinking shows a continuing struggle between his bourgeois heart and his rebellious mind. His rationalism led him to atheism, materialism, and anarchy, his bourgeois heart led him to virtue, humanitarianism, and the defense of private property. He never formed a reconciliation between the two sides of his nature. So Diderot is often contradictory and confused, but he did see the complexity of life, truth, and right. *D'Alembert's Dream* and several related works, were not printed till after Diderot's death, and so had no influence on contemporary thought.

Diderot continued to write short stories, some of which are

excellent pieces of realism, of incisive characterization, of closely knit construction, and great economy of means. He has been credited by some critics with being the creator of the modern short story, "a form of writing," says one critic, "characterized by the utmost concentration of all means toward a single effect."

As early as 1759, Diderot had considered selling his large library partly to provide his daughter with a dowry. Catharine the Great of Russia heard about Diderot's desire to sell his books, and she made him a very good offer. At the same time, Catharine allowed Diderot to keep his books until she might want them, and set aside a stipend he was to receive as librarian of his collection. Diderot gladly accepted the offer, and entered into extended correspondence with the Russian Empress. Diderot did some purchasing for her of art objects at auctions in Paris, and recommended several artists and scholars whom Catharine invited to her court in Saint Petersburg. In 1773, after repeated invitations, Diderot went himself to visit Catharine. Each was delighted with the other, and they spent long hours in conversation. Catharine said to him, "Sometimes you seem to have the head of a man a hundred years old, at other times that of a child of twelve." The members of the court were, in general, unfriendly. The courtiers were shocked by Diderot's informal manners, were suspicious of his radical theories, and were jealous of the favor he enjoyed. Finally, after nearly six months, Diderot grew so homesick for his friends in Paris, even for his wife with whom he always quarreled, that he left for home. But the Russian episode remained the great adventure of Diderot's life. He returned richer in experience and with broadened horizons.

Diderot's most important work for Catharine the Great was his treatise on education, *Plans for a University*. Here he advocated a national system of free education with special subsidies for impoverished students. Diderot showed a preference for modern languages and science as against the emphasis on religious philosophy common in the church schools of his day. "I think," he wrote, "we should give in the schools an idea of all the knowledge necessary to a citizen, from legislation to the mechanical arts." Diderot was the first to see the importance of technical studies in the civilization that the new science was beginning to create. He sees the trend of education away from schools for the few toward a democratic education for the entire nation. It was all, says one unfriendly critic, "a revolt against Jesuit education the purpose of which was to place the mask of the gentleman over the essential wickedness of human nature."

In some of the essays written for Catharine the Great, Diderot shows his preference for democratic political institutions. He believes in some measure of popular representation and the correction of current abuses in taxation and administration. Diderot denounces benevolent despotism. He calls for a better balance between the different sections of society, and insists on the more equal distribution of wealth. Like the Physiocrats who influenced him, he held that agriculture should be favored over industry. Diderot's dream was of "an egalitarian nation of small property owners, virtuous like the Roman

Republic." He warns, though, against the weaknesses of the common people who are stupid until they are educated and learn to use their reason. Diderot, like the other Philosophes, looked to the American colonies as the great hope of mankind, where men could profit from the mistakes of the past and build a society based on reason. And he welcomed the American Revolution when it came, though, like the other Philosophes, he had an incomplete knowledge of American conditions.

One of Diderot's later works that attracted attention was the story of *Jacques the Fatalist.* Inspired partly by Sterne's *Tristam Shandy* and partly by Rabelais, he weaves together in an imaginary conversation between two travellers, a fascinating comment covering many aspects of human affairs. The theme of the book is the acceptance of experience against all abstract formulas. As in his other works, Diderot denied free will, and held that virtue will find strong support in the good opinion of men. If you are good you will be loved, and, if bad, hated. Conscience, experience, and reason will show the path to the good life. It is an entertaining and stimulating book which greatly appealed to Goethe, Carlyle, and Stendhal.

Except for the *Encyclopedia*, Diderot produced only an unsystematic and disjointed body of writing. He followed the current of his time in scorning systematic philosophy. Diderot, though he was not a great writer, was one of the most fertile and suggestive thinkers of the Eighteenth Century. He did at least produce the materials for a philosophy of materialism, though he was always able to overflow the tight bounds of materialism and to admit its limitations. As a stylist, Diderot was often exaggerated in expression, and declamatory, and, as with Voltaire, many of the abuses he attacked have passed away, and the ideas he espoused have become commonplaces.

In his old age, Diderot said of himself, "I am not conscious of having made use of half my powers; I have only fiddle-faddled." He had always spent a great deal of time talking to an endless stream of visitors who came to him for advice, and on revising manuscripts sent for him to read. Grimm wrote of Diderot, after Diderot's death, he was, "a rare man who would have immortalized himself by twenty masterpieces, had he known how to be more miserly of his time, and not abandoned it to a thousand people." This, however, is probably not true, for Diderot seems to have been incapable of sustained thought. His role was greater than his work; all his writings are suggestive; many are stimulating, but neither in content nor style did he produce a great masterpiece.

Diderot's own age regarded him first as a conversationalist. One who knew him well wrote, "his face shining with the fire of inspiration, Diderot spread his light to all minds, his warmth to all hearts. He who has known Diderot only in his own writings has not known him. His discussion was always animated, perfectly sincere, subtle without obscurity, varied in its forms, brilliant in imagination, and fertile in ideas. I have experienced no greater intellectual pleasure."

2. *The Encyclopedia*

The *Encyclopedia* was Diderot's masterpiece. As editor, he slaved for over twenty years finding contributors, often having to rewrite their articles, writing several hundred articles himself, on subjects from philosophy to the mechanical arts, contending with the opposition of Church and state, the desertion of some of his friends, the treachery of the publisher, and finally ruining his eyes reading endless proofs. Diderot declared his purpose in all this when he said he "wanted to change the general way of thinking." It was to be a great compendium of scientific, technical, and historical knowledge with a strong tone of criticizing society and its institutions and spreading rational and scientific ideas. It aimed to be both popular and learned. All the Philosophes contributed; Voltaire wrote on *Esprit* and literature, Montesquieu on taste, Buffon on nature, Turgot on philosophy and economics, and Rousseau on music. Voltaire declared he would be glad to be even the errand-boy of the *Encyclopedia*.

The idea of an encyclopedia was, by no means, a new one. The Middle Ages had produced several encyclopedias, including the great *Speculum* of Vincent of Beauvais. The Sixteenth, Seventeenth, and early Eighteenth Centuries had seen the appearance of a number of encyclopedias, including some general histories of thought of an encyclopedia nature. Also other encyclopedias had been projected including one by Bacon, one by Leibniz, and another by Locke. Many of these early modern encyclopedias were English in origin. In 1728 and 1729 an Englishman named Chambers had published a two volume

Cyclopedia or *Universal Dictionary of the Arts and Sciences.*
Though written by one man, it was more thorough than earlier encyclopedias, was supplied with many cross references,
and went through five editions in eighteen years. A leading
French publisher, Le Breton, proposed to bring out a translation in French. It was to consist of four volumes of text and a
volume of illustrations. And Le Breton got permission from
the government to publish it.

Before anything was done, Le Breton planned to revise the
work and extend it to ten volumes. In 1745 Le Breton called
in d'Alembert and Diderot as advisors. After a time, the publisher decided to ask Diderot to be chief editor. The publisher
did this because he respected Diderot's range of learning and
his knowledge of English. In 1747 Diderot was appointed
editor in chief with d'Alembert as an assistant in charge of
mathematics. Diderot accepted the position because it assured
him of an income with which to support his family. It was Diderot who proposed to the publisher that, instead of translat-
ing Chambers' *Cyclopedia*, that a new and original work be
undertaken.

Diderot wrote to the publisher, "The French are great
enough to write their own encyclopedia! My plan is to do
something never before attempted. No one man, in a brief
lifetime, can possibly embrace all knowledge. We will have
each subject treated by the most eminent specialist in the field.
Our encyclopedia will be not only the best work of its kind,
but the greatest collaborative enterprise in the history of
mankind, a synthesis of French genius, the monument of our

century." These words were very prophetic, and it showed Diderot as a man possessed of a great vision. Fortunately, the publisher immediately realized the possibilities of this novel idea, and saw for himself great financial possibilities.

It was agreed that the work would be in eight volumes, which later stretched to seventeen, with at least six hundred plates, which later extended to eleven volumes of plates. The plates, on which Diderot insisted, were to be largely devoted to industrial processes, a subject never before handled so completely in encyclopedias. Articles and plates on industrial processes proved, in the end, to be hard to obtain. Many technical processes had been passed down from one worker to another, and nobody had bothered to write about them. Also methods of manufacture were often kept secret, jealously guarded from business rivals and the tax collector. The articles should be thorough, and connected with cross references so as to gather together much of man's scattered knowledge. For this task, no man was better fitted than Diderot. He had a wide range of knowledge of many fields, and was a man of great energy and enthusiasm.

To d'Alembert, Diderot assigned the task of making a system of classifying the articles to be collected, and of writing the introduction. This introduction was a brilliant short history of human accomplishment based on the theory that knowledge gained through observation and experience is responsible for all man's progress. It was even more a manifesto, than an introduction, though it showed d'Alembert's caution and timidity. The idea of the encyclopedia caught on among the Philosophes, and it was not difficult to get collaborators. The project of the *Encyclopedia* soon became a favorite topic of conversation in the salons. It was already conceived as a great organ waging war on ignorance, superstition, and all sorts of current abuses. In the prospectus, written by Diderot, he described the usefulness of a work that would cover the liberal arts, the sciences, and the mechanical arts. It would take the place of a whole library. The arrangement would not be strictly alphabetical but would be classified by the mental faculty on which they depend, as memory, reason, and imagination. No biographical articles would be included. The purpose of the work, Diderot declared, was "to assemble all knowledge scattered over the earth's surface, to assure that the works of the past centuries will not have been useless work in the centuries to come, and that our descendants, better educated, may be happier."

The articles began to pour in. In general, they advocated a secular morality, having human happiness in this life as its object. Great emphasis was laid from the earliest contributions on toleration and humanitarianism. The first two volumes attracted great attention and drew two thousand subscribers. Then the government ordered the work suppressed. But the work went on secretly. In one volume d'Alembert wrote an article on *Geneva* in which the liberty of thought there was lauded, but in which the author urged Geneva to establish a theater. This brought into publication a *Letter to d'Alembert* by Rousseau in which he attacked the idea of a theater in Geneva as tending to bring in luxury and vice. The letter of Rous-

seau alienated both Voltaire and Diderot. The censorship of
the first seven volumes, later caused the cautious d'Alembert
to withdraw from the enterprise. D'Alembert was characterized by Sainte-Beuve as, "prudent, circumspect, and moderate
in doctrine, timid in temperament, but a skeptic in everything
except geometry." The censorship by the government of the
first two volumes and the threatened withdrawal of d'Alembert had been heavy blows to Diderot. But he was encouraged
by the public reception of the first volumes. Pirated editions of
the work began to appear, its fame spread all across Europe,
even to Russia, and it soon had four thousand three hundred
subscribers.

Looked at from the point of view of the present, the tone of
the first two volumes, as of all those that followed, seems relatively mild. There was no overt and head-on attack of the
cardinal mysteries of the orthodox Christian faith, and no direct denunciation of the abuses of the Church. But much was
said on these subjects by innuendo and by the vigorous advo-
cacy of toleration and freedom of thought. Insolent allusions
to sacred matters were concealed in unlikely places. Attacks on
pagan religions implied criticisms of Christianity; the article
on Juno, for example, cast doubt on the legend of the Virgin
Mary. The Franciscans are praised in one article, but mocked
in another. The article on God is orthodox, but the entry *Demonstration* would lead to contradictory conclusions. At the
same time articles on the contradictions in the Bible and in
the history of dogma and ritual were set down by a simple
exposition of facts. Commonly expressed was the idea that the

common people ought to be the main concern of government. All sorts of abuses in the government were described in a straight-forward manner.

By 1757, seven volumes had been published, most of them in secret. Again the government, urged on by the Church, intervened to forbid circulation of the work, and, for a time, it looked as though the whole project would have to be dropped. D'Alembert and Turgot withdrew, but Diderot decided to keep on working in secret. And finally the last ten volumes were brought out at the same time, and escaped censorship.

In science, the *Encyclopedia* praised the use of observation and experiment, and pushed for its triumph over Scholasticism and purely rationalist schools of thought. It popularized the theories and the applications of science, and promised future scientific progress. The work led to increasing respect for the trades and for those occupied with them. "Put on one side of the scales," wrote Diderot, "the real advantages of the most sublime sciences and of the most honored arts, and on the other side those of the mechanical arts, and you find that more praise has been given to the men who were busy in making us believe that we were happy than to the men who were concerned in causing us to be really happy. How queer our judgments are! We require that people should be usefully employed, and we despise useful men." This was a strong note of utilitarianism and of glorification of the middle and working classes.

Along with science and technology, the *Encyclopedia* emphasized nature, reason, and tolerance. In this it appealed to all but the most Conservative readers. Some of the most controversial articles that involved these ideas give arguments on both sides of the question. By innuendo, religions were attacked, tolerance preached, and a morality based on human experience and independent of religion set forth. Blunt materialism and determinism were excluded, but Locke's theory of sensations was often repeated, and this was a dissolvent to any religious authority based simply on revelation.

In politics, tyranny was condemned, the social contract, and the right to revolt were defended. The state exists to protect the rights of the individual. Governments are created for the needs of men, and these are best protected in a limited monarchy, and reforms in the tax system are advocated. The *Encyclopedia* contained many articles on the arts and letters, and, in a crude way, it laid the foundations of modern sociology, anthropology, and ethnology. It contained useful information of these subjects, and gave an impulse to further investigations. There was, on the other hand, little understanding of social facts as apart from the individual, and the abstractions of rationalist explanation take the place of the limited findings of scientific investigation.

The articles are often superficial. As one writer said, "People want to be well-informed about all things but with the least possible trouble to themselves; that is the most notable thing about this age of ours." There are many repetitions in the articles, and many articles contradicted each other. The bulk of the work was done by hacks, and it often merely repeated earlier work. The *Encyclopedia* contained many inac-

curacies of fact, and also compromises with truth to avoid the
censorship. Many other works expressed a more advanced
stage of French thought.

The *Encyclopedia*, as a whole, united the Philosophes into
one party, and was a rallying point of their ideas. A great blow
had been struck at obscurantist despotism in both Church and
state. The right of the common man, guided by reason, to be
more master of his fate had been declared with an emphasis
which no longer brooked permanent denial. The right of reason to follow its discoveries was laid down with a force that
has ever since put their opponents on the defensive. In spite
of the Jesuits, the Jansenists, the clergy, the Parlement of
Paris, the government and a great part of the court; in spite of
the pamphlets, sermons, and books refuting them, and in spite
of the indifference of the masses, the Philosophes had won! A
Trojan Horse had been planted square in the middle of the
Old Regime!

6

OTHER FRENCH REFORMERS

1. The Physiocrats

The Physiocrat School of French Economists have substantial claims to be regarded as the real founders of economics in the modern sense. They were called the Physiocrats because they held that the basis of national wealth was in agriculture. They believed that the problem of wealth, the conditions of production, and the laws of distribution are matters to which scientific and precise reasoning may be applied with the object of arriving at universal truths. Like the other Philosophes, they held that there were natural laws which govern human actions, and the problem was to find the economic structure of society that would accord with these natural economic laws. These natural laws were held to be superior to the laws of man's making.

There is fundamentally a right of everyone to that portion of things a man can obtain by his own labor. So private property is consecrated on the basis of labor, and the state should guarantee liberty of contract. The primary function of positive laws is the enforcement of natural laws which are imprinted on the hearts of men. Thus, the less economic legislation the better. So they arrived at the idea of non-interference of the state in economic affairs, which came to be known as the doctrine of *laissez-faire.*

A number of critics in the Age of Louis XIV had criticized the Mercantilist ideas and the policies of Colbert and of Louis XIV. These were the precursors of the Physiocrats. Voltaire had early preached the ideas of free enterprise and the freedom of trade, and had pointed out that the prosperity of England and Holland was the result of trade unfettered by a lot of government regulations.

The leading Physiocrat was Quesnay (1694-1774). He was the son of a lawyer and small landowner, and was raised on a farm in the Ile de France. At sixteen, he was apprenticed to a surgeon, and later studied medicine in Paris. He was very successful as a physician, and became the court doctor of Mme. de Pompadour and of Louis XV. Though Quesnay published little he gradually drew a group of followers about him. They greatly revered Quesnay and called him "the Confucius of Europe." Among his disciples were Turgot and the Marquis of Mirabeau, the father of the leader in the early phase of the French Revolution.

Quesnay's basic ideas were the primacy of agriculture as the source of national wealth, and the existence of natural economic laws of supply and demand. To Quesnay, economics was an exact science, the principles of which were "susceptible of demonstration as severe and incontestable as those of geometry and algebra." At the age of sixty-two, Quesnay published his *Economic Table.* He had already published articles on *Grains* and *Farmers* in the *Encyclopedia,* and was known through the publications of some of his disciples. The *Economic Table* has always seemed a vast mystification, but Quesnay's followers regarded it as almost a religious revelation. The *Table* tried to show how wealth flowed through a community, and that the economic health of a community depended on exactly how it flowed. It indicated how wealth passed from one class of society to another, and why it always followed the same route.

Quesnay and the Physiocrats started with the assumption that agriculture alone is truly productive—a vast simplification. It should be remembered, at the time, France was primarily agricultural. It had the largest area of fertile land in Western or Central Europe, and the vast majority of its people were engaged in agriculture. Also France's richest citizens were those who owned large landed estates. At the time, agriculture, commerce, and industry were all burdened with a mass of governmental regulations. Among the many interferences with free economic activity were the internal customs boundaries within France which Turgot attacked as "remnants of Gothic barbarism."

The Physiocrats were disdainful of history, and anything in their own world that did not fit in with their ideas. They went so far as to class all economic activities, except those of agriculture, as unproductive and sterile. "It is agriculture," declared Quesnay, "which furnishes all the material of industry and commerce." The Physiocrats speak, at times, as if the commercial classes were scarcely a part of the nation at all. For agriculture to be profitably pursued it should be freed from all government regulations and should best be conducted on a large scale. Free and improve agriculture and that would raise taxes, and this would relieve the growing financial distress of the state.

Quesnay distinguished three classes in society. First, a productive class of farmers with whom he would also class fishermen and miners; next, a proprietary class of managers which would include the large landowners, and, last, a sterile class of merchants, manufacturers, domestic servants, and members of the professions. The Physiocrats laid down rules for the large landed proprietors. They should continue to bring new lands into cultivation without neglecting lands already cultivated. They must act as stewards of society disposing of the wealth which nature has produced in such a way as to further the general interest. They should devote their leisure to gratuitous services to society and to the state. They must aid and protect their tenants, and, finally, as the Physiocrats believed in a single tax on land which all land owners must pay, as the only justifiable tax, they must help to bear the economic burdens of the state.

Throughout society, the interests of the nation are best served by the free and untrammeled economic self-interest of individuals each working for his own profit. So by following his own interest the individual would further the good of everybody else. The Physiocrats believed society could run itself alone once the clumsy machinery of state interference was abolished. The state should protect the natural liberty which the buyer has to buy and the seller to sell. Freedom of competition among buyers and sellers is a sufficient guarantee against any abuse. Complete liberty can alone assure the sellers of a price capable of encouraging production, and give the buyer the best product at the lowest price. They saw no social problem except to get rid of the economic regulations which existed.

The Physiocrats believed in enlightened despotism provided it was enlightened enough to get rid of all government economic regulations. Government should make its actions conform to the laws of nature. Since there is only one source of national wealth, namely agriculture, all taxation should be imposed on land. The two great functions of government to the Physiocrats were to uphold the right of private property, and to release individual economic initiative by removing all artificial barriers. Governments could also contribute to the general welfare by extending education which would teach men the laws of nature, by building roads and canals, and by adapting the ruler's needs to meet the taxes collected. To the Physiocrats, the state becomes a kind of "passive policeman." The sole art of government is not to make new laws but to maintain a condition in which the laws of nature could operate freely.

Many rulers were influenced by the ideas of the Physiocrats: the Margrave of Baden, the Grand Duke of Tuscany, Joseph II of Austria, Catharine the Great of Russia, and the Kings of Poland and Sweden. In France, the rapid increase in wealth and prosperity, at least for the more well-to-do, which marked the half century before the Revolution, was to some extent due to the Liberal economic legislation which followed the ideas of the Physiocrats.

2. Some Minor Philosophes

Among the lesser Philosophes there was a great deal of writing and publication though generally each writer was best known through one important work.

The Abbé de Saint-Pierre (1658-1743) did much of his writing during the reign of Louis XIV, but his visionary schemes and his doctrinaire attitudes relate him more to the Age of the Philosophes. Though he was a pupil of the Jesuits, he became a fierce antagonist of religious intolerance and believed in a natural religion. He studied physics and medicine in Paris, and was a close friend of Fontenelle. The Abbé visited regularly certain salons in Paris, and was elected to the French Academy from which, however, he was later ejected for having criticized Louis XIV. He joined the famous *Club de L'Entresol* where he met Montesquieu. The Abbé favored enlightened despotism, but believed it should be tempered by a complex system of advisory councils and by an academy of forty experts appointed by the King on the basis of nominations from the magistrates, the clergy, and the nobility.

The Abbé invented a long series of schemes for increasing man's happiness. He proposed one reform program after another: for a graduated land tax, for reducing the number of law suits, for reforming spelling, for ridding the seas of pirates, for the establishment of an official press, for suppressing begging, for building new roads and canals, for stopping dueling, for a central postal system, and for a national system of schools which would include the professional and vocational training of children and the elimination of most of the inequities between the sexes in education. The Abbé de Saint-Pierre was perhaps the first systematic Utilitarian. "The value," he wrote, "of a book, of a regulation, of an institution, or of any public work is proportioned to the number of the actual pleasures which it produces for the greatest number of men."

The Abbé de Saint-Pierre was sent as a French delegate to the Peace Congress of Utrecht. And out of this experience he came to write his most famous work, *A Project to Fix Perpetual Peace in Europe.* The work was based in part on ideas of Henry IV and Sully, and those of Grotius. The rulers of different countries were to sign a pact to renounce all claims against one another. Military establishments were to be reduced, and kept only in a limited form. If disputes broke out, they were to be referred to a meeting of the nations for arbitration. A European court of justice, and an international European army were to be created. By these means, Europe would become a friendly association of law-abiding and peace-loving nations.

The Abbé was regarded as a hopeless visionary and a sort of privileged nuisance. But Rousseau reworked his ideas in one of his writings, and so did Kant. And a few of the Abbé's ideas were embodied in the League of Nations and the United Nations. Some of the Abbé's ideas were not of his invention but were common among the Philosophes who set up the ideal of a cosmopolitan and humanitarian culture. They regarded all manifestations of nationalism as irrational and unnatural, and as harmful to human welfare. As Dr. Johnson said, "patriotism is the last refuge of a scoundrel." So these ideas were in the air in the Eighteenth Century. The sum and substance of this Eighteenth Century cosmopolitanism is well summed up in Goethe's statement, "above the nations is humanity."

La Mettrie (1709-1751) was an anatomist and a physician who studied in Paris and Leyden. Then he spent some time at the Court of Frederick the Great, and was elected a member of the Berlin Academy. He was not very original, but was very outspoken. Among a number of his works, *Man a Machine* was best known. Le Mettrie maintained that both men and animals are machines, the only difference being in the complexity of organization. He shows that the human mind is affected by physical conditions as by fever and drugs, by a blow on the head, by sleep, and by food. The transition from man to animals and from animals to plants is gradual. The superiority of the mind of man over that of the other animals is due to man's capacity for symbolic reasoning. Ethics are manmade, arbitrary, and corrupted by priests and by the selfishness of the ruling classes. Pleasure is the mainspring of conduct.

The soul is an empty term that has no meaning. La Mettrie regarded metaphysical speculation as folly, and was a complete exponent of pure materialism. Atheism is the only means of assuring the happiness of men which has long been rendered impossible by the wars of words brought on by the theologians. Religion is hostile to science and reason, has no effect on morals, and is useful only to politicians and priests.

La Mettrie in a number of works became the chief exponent among the Philosophes of an untempered materialism.

As La Mettrie's works were the most blatant expression of materialism, the writings of the Baron d'Holbach (1723-1789) represented the strongest statement of atheism. Holbach was a German nobleman who preferred to live in Paris, and his culture was almost entirely French. He was wealthy and entertained lavishly all the Philosophes and many important foreign visitors especially those from Britain. Holbach, said one Philosophe, "keeps the cafe of Europe." In his writings, Holbach attacks both the fears and the hopes raised by religion as well as all intolerance and persecution. For the *Encyclopedia* he wrote nearly three hundred articles on physics, chemistry, natural history, mineralogy, and metallurgy. In 1767 he published *Christianity Unveiled* in which he attacked all religion as the great source of human evils. Four years later he brought out his principal work, the *System of Nature*, in which he had probably been assisted by his atheist friend, Diderot. Here he preaches stark atheism. The faithful, declared Holbach, "offer up to heaven vows, sacrifices, and presents to obtain the end of their suffering, which, in reality, are due only to the negligence, ignorance, and perversity of their guides, the folly of their institutions, their silly customs, false opinions, irrational laws, and above all to the want of knowledge." "Men," he goes on, "will be good when they are well instructed, well governed, and when they are punished or despised for the evil, and justly rewarded for the good they do their fellow creatures. In short, does not everything prove that morality and virtue are totally incompatible with the notions of God whom his ministers and interpreters have described in every country as the most capricious, unjust, and cruel of tyrants? To learn the true principles of morality, men have no need of theology, of revelation, or gods. They have need only of reason. Let us persuade men to be just, beneficent, moderate, and sociable, not because the gods demand it but because they must please men. Let us advise them to abstain from vice and crime, not because they will be punished in the other world, but because they will suffer for it in this." All in all, Holbach delivered the most telling attack against organized Christianity as a series of propositions offered for rational belief.

Holbach saw nothing in the universe but matter in spontaneous movement. What men call the soul becomes extinct as soon as the body dies. Happiness and the avoidance of pain are the end of mankind. The restraints of religion should be replaced by an education which would develop an enlightened self-interest. The study of science should bring human desires into accordance with nature which Holbach identifies with reason and utility. Politics should aim at giving the advantages of society to the greatest number, an idea also held by the Abbé de Saint-Pierre, by Helvétius and later by Bentham. Holbach hated arbitrary despotism, and believed only in a benevolent rule. The populace has the right to revolt against arbitrary government. He believed strongly in free speech, and he favored a system of representative government in which the right to vote would be confined to men of property who alone had a stake in the country. Holbach also believed in free trade since nature had decreed that the surplus of one nation would supply the deficiency of another. And he attacked the cruel treatment of prisoners. Differences in wealth in the state should be proportioned to social usefulness. In the life of man there is no room for a final cause, for chance, or free will.

Holbach's style is very diffuse, and he asserts rather than proves his statements. He published a series of works to expound his ideas. All of his writings were published either anonymously or under assumed names, and all were printed outside France. Holbach's writings caused a kind of crisis among the Philosophes; the more timid became frightened at the extent to which reason had carried him. His atheism annoyed Voltaire, and shocked Rousseau. Voltaire feared atheism because it would deprive the poor and uneducated of superstitions that help to maintain order in society. Rousseau thought it destroyed the spirit and denied the most sacred emotions, and Frederick the Great wrote a refutation of one of Holbach's works, the *Essay on Prejudices.*

Holbach's system said d'Alembert would be excellent if there were no such thing as history. "The Philosophes," said one critic, "never dreamed that if men were offered the truth they would not leap for it, that if they were told ugly facts they would prefer pleasant lies, that if reasonable ideas were offered them they would continue to act as their fathers had done; they did not see that the follies of the past were not only imposed but ingrained, that men carry history not only on their backs but in their heads."

Closely related to the thought of Holbach was that of Helvétius (1715-1771). Helvétius was of German-Swiss ancestry; his grandfather had settled in Paris as a doctor of medicine, and his father was physician to the Queen of France. He became a farmer-general of revenues, and at age of thirty-six retired to write. He had become a man of great wealth; he travelled a great deal in England and Germany, and maintained a famous salon. The only work Helvétius published during his lifetime was *On The Mind* which represents the extreme form of the utilitarian point of view in Eighteenth Century French thought. Helvétius was a materialist who believed men were formed by physical sensations, and by social experience including education. Men are born essentially the same, and most differences are due to environment and education. His basic idea is that men regard as good what brings pleasure and as bad that which brings pain. Men act only from self-interest. "They make so much ado about Helvétius," declared Mme. du Deffand, "because he has revealed everybody's secret." Here Helvétius harks back to ideas of the Calvinists, the Jansenists, and Hobbes. Helvétius was almost the only Philosophe that did not believe in the goodness of human nature.

Helvétius *On the Mind* shocked and disgusted Rousseau. *On The Mind* was censured by the Sorbonne, by the Pope, and by the Parlement of Paris, and it was burned by the public executioner. Even Diderot refuted the work, by declaring Helvétius' reasoning was often superficial and his judgments inaccurate. Voltaire scorned the book, as full of commonplaces, and added that what little was original was false or doubtful. The work, however, later influenced Bentham and John Stuart Mill.

Condillac (1714-1780) was the most systematic thinker among the Philosophes, though he was not very original. As a youth, Condillac received a theological education. He hated, as did the other Philosophes, speculative metaphysics. The great influences on him, as on many of the other Philosophes, were those of Locke and Newton. Philosophy is only useful when it uses the methods of science. Condillac's best known work was his *Treatise on the Sensations* of 1754. Here he followed Locke's ideas, and went further to prove even memory, imagination, judgment, and reflection are nothing but transformed sensations. Men differ in the vividness of their five senses and in their power of judgment. Condillac's position leads straight to materialism, determinism, and atheism. To illustrate his ideas, Condillac imagines a statue perceives a succession of odors; it develops, in turn, attention, pleasure or pain, memory, judgment, imagination, passions, and other faculties of the mind. Then the author endows his statue successively with hearing, taste, sight, and touch. As a result, the ideas in the mind become more complex until a full supply of human ideas is attained. His theory is the most elaborate attempt to reduce all the processes of the mind to passive experience. Unlike some of his contemporaries, Condillac wrote lucidly and with moderation. And he is one of the founders of modern psychology.

The idea of progress—what was later to be called "the gospel of perfectibility"—first attracted wide attention in the later Seventeenth Century in the famous quarrel between "Ancients" and "Moderns." But the idea of progress in human affairs was itself older, and was really the work of early modern scientists who believed in the social usefulness of their discoveries. The Renaissance Humanists had put the golden age in the remote past of Greece and Rome, and the religious reformers had found the golden age in the time of Jesus and Saint Paul. It was the early modern scientists who put the golden age in the future. Beginning in the Fifteenth Century, the progress of scientific discovery had been remarkable, and this progress continued during the age of the Enlightenment in the Eighteenth Century. One important discovery after another was being made as the Philosophes were writing. The idea of progress became to some a sort of religious faith that the conditions of human life steadily become better, that each generation is better off than its predecessors, and that this progress will continue into the future.

The greatest prophet of progress in the Enlightenment was Condorcet (1743-1794) though he sums up what others had thought rather than creating anything very new. He belonged to an old aristocratic family and was a marquis. He was educated by the Jesuits, and his first writings were on mathematics. He was elected to the Academy of Sciences and to the French Academy. But in the French Revolution, he repudiated all clerical and aristocratic ideas. He served in the Legislative Assembly and in the Convention. But finally he was proscribed along with the Girondists during the Reign of Terror. He went into hiding, and, rather than face execution when captured, took poison.

While in hiding, Condorcet wrote his principal work, *A Sketch for an Historical Picture of the Progress of the Human Race*. Here he presents a survey of human history, that represents a series of successive steps in the advancement of mankind. The laws of progress, which would extend into the future, were as constant as the laws of science. Progress is due to the spread of science and reason which enable men better to control their environment. Condorcet thought that the march of progress might slow up, but he does not recognize that it will ever go backward. "The result of my work," Condorcet wrote, "will be to show, by reasoning and by facts, that there is no limit to the perfecting of the powers of man; that human perfectibility is in reality indefinite, that the progress of this perfectibility, henceforth independent of any power that might wish to stop it, has no other limit than the duration of the globe upon which nature has placed us. Doubtless this progress can proceed at a pace more or less rapid, but it will never go backward." For the future, Condorcet advocated woman's suffrage, the equality of the rights of men and women including the equality of husband and wife before the law, co-education, civil marriage, divorce, and birth control. Condorcet marked ten phases in the history of human progress; nine of these were in the past or present, and the tenth would be in the future.

Condorcet's illusion, like that of some of the other Philosophes, was to suppose that the evil propensities of men would disappear with the traditional forms and institutions through which they functioned. They did not realize that the wiping-out of old oppressions and inequities often did little more than make room for new ones.

3. Early Socialists

At the extreme left of the camp of the Philosophes were a few writers of Socialist outlook such as the Abbé Mably, (1709-1785). After receiving an elementary education by the Jesuits, he studied theology, then served as a secretary at the royal court from 1741 to 1748. This gave him an insight into affairs of state. In his reading, he was influenced by Plato, Cicero, Locke, and by his brother, Condillac. He became firmly convinced that psychology, ethics, and politics were all to be understood as aspects of natural law—a favorite theme of the Philosophes. And the first dictate of natural law was the equality of all men. Men should not only be equal in society, but there could be no genuine equality without economic equality. Mably believed Communism the ideal system, and that it had probably prevailed among primitive men. He was, however, moderate in his actual program for reforms.

Private property, Mably held, is the root of all social troubles, and private property should be restricted. He stopped short of advocating state ownership, but proposed a series of practical reforms: laws restricting industry and commerce, improved penal and legal codes, stern inheritance laws, and universal state education. He believed in calling the Estates General, and he laid out plans for framing a new constitution for France. Mably's principal works were *On the Rights and Duties of a Citizen* and *On Legislation.* He predicted the coming of the French Revolution, and Robespierre consulted his works for inspiration. Mably, however, was very pessimistic, and believed men would never be better.

Related in thought to Mably was Morelly though he was less read than Mably. Almost nothing is known about the facts of his life. In his writings, Morelly held that in the ideal state no private property except that necessary for individual daily wants was to be permitted. Every citizen was to be a public servant working for the state according to a detailed code which prescribed down to the smallest detail the behavior of the entire population. His best known work was his *Code of Nature* which influenced Babeuf and anticipated many of the ideas of Fourier. Morelly showed himself a violent enemy of the whole economic order of Eighteenth Century France. He painted primitive man as socially minded and virtuous. It was feebleness which originally brought man to form society, and this primitive society was communistic. Men, however, fell from this happy condition through the institution of private property. The environment and not the nature of man had produced the evils of society. Change the environment and man will be happier. Men should return to a communal regime, and above all abolish private property.

Morelly deals first in denunciation of present evils then in elaborately detailed plans for reform. He lays down rules as axioms for reform which, "would cut off at the root the vices and evils of society." "Nobody," he declares, "will own anything in society individually except the things he is currently using for his needs, his pleasures, and his daily work. Every citizen will be a public person, supported, maintained, and employed at public expense. For his part, every citizen will contribute to the public weal in accordance with his strength, his talents, and his age." The nation was to be divided into families, tribes, and garden-cities of the same size. Each city will have a public square around which will be arranged shops and assembly halls. Beyond this will be the residential sections of the garden-city regularly divided by parallel streets. Each tribe will occupy one quarter, and each family a building. There will also be workshops, a hospital, and a prison. And the detailed descriptions and regulations go on for pages.

Morelly's communism can be traced back to Plato, to St. Thomas More, and to the Anabaptists, but it contained many details which he seems to have invented. His chief aim was to form a more moral society. As long as men based their society on self-interest, struggle, unhappiness, and chaos was inevitable. Harmony would only take place if society were deliberately organized on a moral basis. Communism was the only solution for all social problems, and communism was the code of nature.

7

A PHILOSOPHE APART,
ROUSSEAU

Rousseau (1712-1778) is the most original of the Philosophes, the most controversial, and the hardest to understand. He shared some of the ideas of the other Philosophes, but his fundamental approach to man and to society was different in emphasis. At the same time, Rousseau was the last of the great writers of the French Enlightenment and the first of a new and different dispensation. His writings are full of superficial contradictions and are sprinkled with paradoxes, and he uses the same word with different meanings. His work, however, does have a fundamental unity. Rousseau always insisted on the unity of his ideas. "I have written," he said, "on diverse subjects, but always on the same principles, always the same morals, the same belief, the same maxims, and the same opinions." And, near the end of his life, he declared his writings were constructed on "a great principle." "The thought of Rousseau," writes one critic, "is by no means one of those systems laid out in advance. It grew and gathered like a flowing river. We must be prepared for ebb and flow, for twists and turns, for cross-currents, and backwaters with a whirl pool here and there."

Rousseau's basic idea, running through his work, is that society had corrupted the natural goodness of man, and only through a better society could man be improved. He wanted to create a civilization worthy of man, and men worthy of such an improved civilization. So in spite of some contradictions, as he moved back and forth from Anarchy to Collectivism, all parts of his thought do basically hold together, supplementing one another. His central doctrine was that man, good by nature, can transform himself into a good citizen in a good society. Rousseau was always trying to see how civilized man can recover the benefits of the natural man without returning to the state of nature and without renouncing the benefits of the social state. He was, also, always anxious to preserve the idea of his innocence and the idea of the goodness of his heart.

1. Early Life

Jean Jacques Rousseau's early life was a life of vagabondage. It was all "a thing of shreds and patches." Nearly all that is known of his early life comes from his autobiography, the *Confessions*. He was born in Geneva, the son of a humble watchmaker. Rousseau always spoke of himself as a "citizen of Geneva," and he remained proud of many of the aspects of the life of his birthplace. His mother died when he was nine days old, and his early education was desultory. Indeed, he was almost entirely self-educated. The early experiences of his life, when he lived on the outer edge of society, played a great role in the formation of his ideas. Emotionally, Rousseau never grew up, and he relived, all through his life, the experiences of his childhood and youth.

Rousseau's father was dissipated and violent tempered. At the age of ten, the boy went to live with his mother's relatives, and then he betook himself to live with an uncle. The uncle apprenticed the youthful Rousseau to a notary who soon dismissed him. Next, he was apprenticed to an engraver. Rousseau liked the work, but ran away because he thought the engraver mistreated him. Then began an extraordinary series of wanderings. He fell in with some Catholic missionaries, and was, for a time, converted to Catholicism. The missionaries sent him to Mme. de Warens, a kind-hearted widow at Annecy. Rousseau, at this time, did not stay long with her, but wandered off to Turin where he first became a footman to a wealthy woman. Soon afterwards, she died, and Rousseau worked a short time for a count. Next, he returned to Mme. de Warens, who though a convert to Catholicism, was a kind of sentimental deist. Mme. de Warens became his mistress, and sent him to school where he studied classics and music. For awhile, he taught music, and then became the secretary to a Greek cleric who was collecting funds to restore the Church of the Holy Sepulchre. This took Rousseau for the first time to Paris. From Paris, he returned on foot to rejoin Mme. de Warens. Next we hear of him as a tutor in Lyons. Rousseau found this work distasteful, and returned to Paris where he tried, in vain, to interest musicians in a new system of musical notation. A friend in Paris got Rousseau the position of secretary to the French ambassador to Venice with whom he stayed eighteen months. The ambassador never treated Rousseau fairly, and he failed to pay Rousseau his full wages. This experience of injustice from such a "civilized" person and the failure of "civilized" Parisians to come to his defense was an experience that later helped to form his ideas in the *Discourse on the Origins of Inequality.*

Next, Rousseau returned to Paris, where he met Diderot with whom he formed a fast friendship. Diderot had much influence on the young man, and introduced him in some of the salons. Rousseau supported himself meagerly by copying music, and he even got an opera of his composition performed privately. He had humiliating experiences with women whose ideal companionship was his constant dream throughout his life, but whose favors he could neither resist nor enjoy without a sense of guilt. In Paris, he met an illiterate woman, a servant in a hotel, with whom he formed an alliance and whom he later married in a ceremony of Rousseau's devising. By her he had five children, all of whom were sent to a home for foundlings. In the meantime, Diderot assigned to Rousseau articles on music for the *Encyclopedia.* Then in 1749 Rousseau suddenly became famous through his *Essay on the Arts and Sciences.*

During these years, Rousseau showed a morbid sensitivity and a love of solitude and of the country. He never cared much for the society of men or for the life of cities. He was very ill-at-ease in the salons where he was received as a kind of curiosity. He was clumsy in manner, meagerly dressed, and uncomfortable in the atmosphere of wit and cynicism. Rousseau was a *petit bourgeois* whose early experiences and habits of mind were utterly at variance from the conventions and traditions of the Paris salons. So his entrance into Parisian society brought him nothing but misery. "Few things," says one critic, "require so much social experience, so much poise and self-reliance, as to enter a clique of clever people who share a common experience and laugh at the same things." Rousseau had none of the necessary qualifications for being a conventional Philosophe. The atheistic views of men like Holbach disgusted him as much as did the formalism of the salon. Vain and sensitive, earnest and sentimental, with no sense of proportion, no capacity for trifling and no sense of humor, and contemptuous of a smooth society that did not recognize his genius, the goodness of his heart, and the purity of his intentions, he could do nothing right. In excitement he rushed to the center of the picture, only to retire within himself bitterly humiliated. The qualities which made Rousseau a social failure also made the friendship he craved impossible. Rousseau only thought of the right thing to say when he was leaving a gathering or after he had left. As a result of his early experiences he was coming to believe that society was all wrong, and to condemn all the partial solutions to problems proposed by the Philosophes.

In part, Rousseau shared an impatience with civilized society and its classical ideas of order and symmetry that were in the air at his time. Sentiment was beginning, all across Europe, to assert its claims. This can be seen in a growing enthusiasm for the simple beauties of nature and of the new world, the purity of the savage as portrayed in the writings of missionaries and travellers, in the growing taste for wild nature and informal gardens. It was already asserting itself in the tearful sentimentality of bourgeois plays and novels. It revealed itself in German Pietism and in the rise of English Methodism both of which sought to stimulate a "religion of the heart." It appeared toward the middle of the century in the work of a whole series of English poets, and in the novels of Richardson, Fielding, Smollett, and Sterne—all of whom became the prophets of sentimentalism which was soon to conquer Europe. Richardson's *Pamela* of 1740 seems to have begun a new age, expressing the grievances and interests of the middle and even the lower classes. With Rousseau this growing sentimentality crystallized into a definite program. He set out to emancipate men from the tyranny of a dry intellectualism and the artificialities of society.

2. The Years of Fame

In 1749, when Rousseau was nearly forty years old, the Academy of Dijon offered a prize on the subject of whether or not the arts and sciences had benefited mankind. Evidently primitivism was in the air or the Academy would never have offered such a prize. Rousseau turned over the question in his mind, and discussed it with Diderot, who, at the time, shared some of Rousseau's ideas. One day when Rousseau was walking from Paris to Vincennes to visit Diderot, who was in prison, he decided to compete for the prize. The form of his answer came to him like a religious conversion. He sat down under a tree, and was swept by wave after wave of emotion. "If ever anything resembled a sudden inspiration," he wrote later, "it was the commotion which began in me. All at once I felt myself dazzled by a thousand sparkling lights; crowds of vivid ideas thronged into my mind with a force and confusion that threw me into unspeakable agitation. I passed half an hour there in such a condition of excitement that when I arose I saw the front of my waistcoat was all wet with tears, though I was wholly unconscious of shedding them. Ah, if ever I could have written a quarter of what I saw and felt under that tree, with what clearness should I have brought out all the contradictions of our social situation; with what simplicity I should have demonstrated that man is naturally good, and that by institutions only is he debased."

The result of all this was Rousseau's *Discourse on the Arts and Sciences* which won him the prize of the Academy of Dijon, and, at the same time, gave him almost instant fame. Man is by nature good. In his primitive condition he was happy and innocent. The misery and corruption prevalent in the modern world are the consequences of the increase of baneful knowledge. There is still more virtue among men of the lower classes than among men of rank and property. "It is under the homespun of the laborer," he declared, "and not beneath the gilt and tinsel of the courtier, that we should look for strength and vigor." And he added, "As the conveniences of life increase, as the arts are brought to perfection and luxury spreads, true courage flags, and virtues disappear." To secure felicity, man must escape to a simpler life. Men in present society exhibit revolting habits of vice, hypocrisy, injustice, and dishonesty. Men have become bad citizens and bad men. Our minds have been corrupted in proportion as our arts and sciences have made advances. Rousseau believed in nature, but refused to approach it by the road of science. Life had taught Rousseau that the promptings of his heart were superior to the logic of his mind. Rousseau's glorification of the natural man runs through all of his later writings.

Here, and still much more in his later writings, Rousseau is saying that we are natural so long as we are true to our own nature. Nature is the test of all our art and ideas, and the right art and thought is to perfect her. The first thing man has is self-love, or what we now would call the instinct of self-preservation. This must always have been natural to men, or they would have perished. The second thing is sympathy or the instinct of mutual help. This has often been set aside through greed and pride. Sympathy, however, is necessary to mitigate the struggle for survival. Conscience must be man's moral guide. And the sole guide for conscience is the faculty of reason. Conscience is the moral force, reason the moral guide. Rousseau neither rejects reason nor does he, like most of the other Philosophes, give reason illimitable sway. There must be a perfect union in which sentiment and reason mutually check and control each other. Man must try to check self-love so as to avoid pride; self-love will seek only what we need, pride will tend to grab at anything whether needed or not. Self-love is satiable, for our needs are limited, pride is insatiable for the false needs a man may conjure up are numberless. To toil upward, man needs one more gift, liberty, and the right of choice. All in all, Rousseau's message is that man must be perfected by sympathy for his fellow men and by reason in accordance with his nature.

Some time afterward, the same Academy of Dijon offered a prize on the effect on civilization of the right of private property. Rousseau again competed, but this time did not win the prize. The result of this second competition was also a work that attracted a tremendous attention and spread Rousseau's fame. This was his *Discourse on The Origins of Inequality*. Here, in an attack on the abuses of private property, Rousseau undermined the whole social system of the Old Regime. Governments should establish social and political institutions in which there are equal rights available to all, and the goodness inherent in the hearts of man will reassert itself.

Rousseau paints primitive men leading a happy carefree life with no needs that cannot be satisfied through instinct. He is full of admiration and sympathy for the savage who is independent and self-sufficient. The state of nature is a state of equality. Then Rousseau traces the steps to a more complex civilization with the growth of private property. "The first man who after enclosing a piece of land," he writes, "said 'this is mine' and found people simple enough to believe him was the real founder of civil society." War, murder, and wretchedness followed. Rich and poor came to be ranged against each other. Evils that had been unknown in a primitive society now became universal.

Throughout, he is trying to show the evils in society that

arise from the rights of property. Rousseau's use of the idea of
a state of nature is, as he says, not an historical concept but a
hypothetical one, a way of illustrating his view of human nature and his description of the ills of society. From private
property, the harmless inequalities which were the outcome
of natural differences gave way to grave social inequalities.
As a result of the inheritance of wealth one class was able to
tyrannize over another. So we see insolent display and insatiable ambition on the one hand, and, on the other, servile trickery and corrupting jealousy. "Men no longer worked to satisfy
real wants, but to get more than others. There is permanent
war between rich and poor." Rousseau did not believe it possible to abolish private property, but he wanted the state to
render its distribution more equal. The *Essay on the Origins
of Inequality* ends with an evocation to the god of simplicity.
Rousseau modifies his primitivism because he realizes that
primitive emotion without reason only leads to self-love running rampant so he did understand that some reason, and that
some civilization was necessary.

These first two essays of Rousseau caused a furore, though
few people took the pains to see exactly what Rousseau said,
but fixed their attention on striking sentences and phrases that
are frequently paradoxical. Rousseau's style was novel, and
this also attracted attention. He was able to evoke moods of
thought and feeling that no other French writer had touched
before. His words and phrases stood for emotional overtones
not present in the clear and rational style of the other Philosophes. Rousseau sent a copy of the book to Voltaire who

thanked Rousseau for "his new book against the human race," and added that reading the book made him "want to walk on all fours, but since I lost the habit more than sixty years before, I feel that it is unfortunately impossible for me to resume it."

Rousseau was always falling in and out of love, and changing his place of residence. For a short time, he held a post as cashier in the receiver-general's office. In 1752 his operetta, the *Village Soothsayer* was presented at Fontainebleau with some success, and he was offered a pension, but out of shyness or pride he refused to appear at court to receive it. Rousseau quarrelled with Diderot, with Voltaire, and with d'Alembert, and he became as obnoxious to the Philosophic coterie as he was to the orthodox, but the public still clamored for his books. He had, moreover, no lack of patrons though he quarrelled with all of them.

In 1760 Rousseau published his popular novel, *Julie* or *The New Heloise.* It is written in the form of letters, and it described the love of a man of low position and a girl of rank, all done in the style of Richardson. The lover is evidently Rousseau in search of an ideal love. The young woman later married a respectable freethinker of her own station. The mental agonies of her rejected lover are fully portrayed, though the distress of both the lover and the beloved are relieved by the influence of noble sentiments, and by the good influence of a philanthropic Englishman. The lover, who is the tutor of the young girl, finally returns to tutor her sons and then dies. The novel was enormously popular; through its emotional style it caused many to weep. Rousseau was now adored by a large circle of readers. The public liked his treatment of love as an ennobling sentiment and of motherhood as an uplifting experience. It reasserted emotion as a valuable force in life, and gave expression to a rising current of sentimentalism, to a feeling for simple virtues, and to the consoling qualities of nature. The novel went through fifty editions before 1789.

In 1762, Rousseau's *Social Contract* was published in Amsterdam. It was intended to be part of a larger work which he never wrote. In the *Social Contract*, Rousseau takes as his fundamental problem the attainment of liberty through political government. A good society is one in which the citizen is both ruler and subject. The natural man is still his ideal, but society and government, though deplorable, are inevitable. "What can render them legitimate," he declared, "I think I can answer." A society of free consent, not of force, a union of each with all on equal terms for the common good, a sovereignty vested in all, and voiced by the general will, this is the heart of his doctrine. The individual must have liberty for progress, but the state that fosters progress must have power to do its work.

Rousseau is, throughout, much influenced by a nostalgia for a Geneva that never existed as he conceived it. Civilized man cannot escape society and government, but must recreate it to recreate himself. Men such as they are not fit for liberty. They must be made fit, and create a type of state that will make them so. The *Social Contract* is a disordered book, Rousseau does not seem to have started out with very clear ideas of his opinions. He never revised the work, and left it with its inconsistencies. Locke and Hobbes had thought of a political contract between ruler and ruled. Rousseau, though borrowing from these English thinkers, thought of a social contract; government was important but secondary. Rousseau's social contract was one by which individual man surrendered their individual wills to be subject to a general will.

In view of Rousseau's position in the two *Discourses* one would expect him to set sharp limits to the rights of society lest it infringe on the rights of the individual. Instead, he ends by glorifying the absolutism of the state and proposing a system of collectivism. He says his problem was "to find a form of association which will defend and protect by the whole common force the person and the goods of each associate, in which each, while uniting himself, with all, will only obey himself, and remain as free as before." The work opens with the striking statement that "Man is born free but is everywhere in chains"—a typical Rousseauistic exaggeration.

Government should never rest on force alone, but on the consent of the governed. He accepts now the idea of private property. Revolution is a possibility, but only as a last resort. The first part of the *Social Contract* is an eloquent defense of liberty and the sovereignty of the people, but the second part, in the name of protecting the sanctity of the general will, becomes a program for a collectivist state.

Rousseau distinguishes between the "general will" and "the will of all." The "general will" is that which is good for all; the "will of all" is the will of the majority. Governments should try to bring about a union of the two. Rousseau classifies governments as monarchy, aristocracy, democracy, and mixed. The least objectional form of government is democracy, but that he believes is only for small states like Geneva. No freedom is possible in a large state unless it is divided into districts and given a federated organization, an organization in which all the citizens could actively participate in the government. In a democracy, there should be periodic assemblies of the sovereign people to determine if the existing form of government is satisfactory, and to find out the pleasure of the people, leaving the administration in the hands of those who have it in charge. Sovereignty always belongs only to the people as a corporate body, while government is merely an agent having delegated powers which can be modified or withdrawn as the will of the people dictates. Coercion in such a state by the will of the majority is not really coercion because when a man individually wants something different from what the social order gives him he is merely capricious, and does not rightly know his own good. Rousseau's conclusion is that in an actual democratic vote the majority can be trusted to know what is really best for all. This is what Rousseau meant by men being "forced to be free." To have the right rule take place, the electorate must be educated. The law coerces the selfish individual and thereby gives him freedom. Rousseau also proposed a civil religion with a few simple dogmas such as the existence of God, the punishment of the wicked, and the sanctity of the social pact and of the law.

The influence of Rousseau's writing on government was to

be far wider in scope and far more persistent than that of Montesquieu and Voltaire for he voiced the aspirations of the masses. He wrote with so much power that he expressed the hopes of men who had no other spokesman. His doctrines, however, were capable of extension and elaboration in directions which would have astonished him. The *Social Contract* was variously interpreted by enthusiasts, endlessly commented on, and triumphantly quoted by rival schools of thought. It has been condemned for an individualism that runs to anarchy and for an absolutism that brings tyranny. There is more Utopian abstraction in the work than practical experience. Rousseau himself said of the *Social Contract*, "Those who boast that they understand the whole of it are cleverer than I am." Redemption for man was possible given the right political institutions. Democracy is the only form of government that offers men and women freedom, and which may, in time, regenerate them, and lead to the formation of a truly good social community.

Also on politics, Rousseau wrote a *Plan for a Constitution for Corsica* (1765), and *Considerations on the Government of Poland* (1772). The work on Corsica follows some of the ideas of the *Social Contract* and is quite Utopian. He declares that the state ought to be the sole owner of property. The work on Poland is much more down to earth, and shows the influence of Montesquieu. He declares that the situation and traditions of Poland make anything like an ideal constitution out of the question. Montesquieu himself could not have been more conservative. Poland should be animated by the spirit of liberty, but the Poles should be moderate in using their liberties. Rousseau advocates a long series of specific reforms including a great emphasis on the extension of education. He justified his cautious advice as a concession to corrupt human nature, an unusual concession for Rousseau. In his suggestions for the government of Poland, Rousseau is the first systematic theorist of a conscious nationalism. He sees Poland as a separate nation with its own peculiar problems.

In 1762, the year of the appearance of the *Social Contract* Rousseau published *Emile or Education* in Amsterdam, a work which immediately attracted a wider circle of readers than had been attracted by the *Social Contract*. Rousseau said the work was "the fruit of twenty years of meditations and of three years of labor." In form, *Emile* was a novel, but actually it was a general treatise on the education of the natural man. "All is well," Rousseau characteristically declared, "when it leaves the hands of the Creator of things, all degenerates in the hands of man." He based his educational ideas on the principle that the child is a developing personality not a small adult. From five to twelve years is a prerational age for the child, when the senses are in the ascendancy, and appeal must be made to concrete experiences. The child should be trained by doing, and by the direct observation of nature. A child should develop as civilization does, from animal to savage and on to a reasoning being. It is foolish to use rote learning and reason on small children since they forget the first, and cannot understand the second.

For children from twelve to fifteen years of age one should

introduce more abstract concepts, then comes training in morality and the facts of sex. Between seventeen and nineteen years of age, the reasoning faculty should be trained, and at twenty the moral sense should be inculcated. Rousseau attacked the use of wet nurses, and started a craze for nursing one's own children. All boys should be taught a craft; Emile chooses that of a carpenter. The child must always be taught to strive for good. Evil exists so that people may have a choice of action. At about eighteen years of age, God must be revealed to the child. So Rousseau outlines a method of developing the natural man "with all the advantages and without any of the vices of civilized men." Everywhere he would allow the child to find the bounds of his own capabilities for himself. The teacher must reason with him only when he is old enough to reason. Emile's education was to end when he married a girl educated in much the same way he had been trained.

Education should encourage rather than restrain most of the natural instincts of the child. In his early years, the child should experience the rigor of things rather than of men, and should suffer only those punishments inflicted by nature herself. Judgment rather than mere knowledge is to be encouraged. The effort of the tutor in the early years of the child is largely negative. The tutor is to see that nothing interferes with the spontaneous development of the faculties of the pupil. Let the child form his own course, let him see with his own eyes, hear with his own ears, and let him feel with his own heart. Let him be governed by no authority except by his own intelligence and experience. The boy must not see a book till he is twelve years old, and his first reading is to be *Robinson Crusoe*. Rousseau had a sublime faith in native intellectual capacity and the innate goodness of human nature. If human relations were ever to be satisfactory, the existing plan of education would have to be changed, and Rousseau pictured the happy results of a natural education that would give men both mastery and freedom, and save them from the miseries he had undergone. It would all serve as the basis for a natural and happy society of free men.

The idea of God is to be taught by seeing God in Nature. And the *Confession of Faith of a Savoyard Vicar* preaches the idea of an emotional sort of deism. The child should be taught that God had made man good, and has planted in him the moral energy to overcome the evils of society not built on natural premises. God has endowed men with conscience to love the good, reason to know it, and liberty to choose it. Rousseau's discussion of religion shows he was religious by temperament, though he believed in no church and no revelation. He recommended reading the Bible, and he believed in God not only as a first cause but also as a God of love. Rousseau was perplexed by the current controversies about science and God, but his heart felt a deep need for faith in God who should sometime repay him for his earthly sufferings. Rousseau's Savoyard Vicar is depicted as a good man and a Catholic priest who after a study of theology had arrived at a natural religion. He had decided that God had created the world, and that man had spoiled nature. Man may, however, improve the condition of this world, and God would reward good and punish evil in a future life. Rousseau taught men to see God in nature where He was best revealed.

The work, while containing many new and useful ideas on education seems utterly impractical. "It is," said one historian, "the most celebrated and influential treatise on education ever written, and the worst." It involves only the tutor and his pupil, and the pupil is to be brought up in complete isolation from other children and other adults. It was most successful in attacking the abstract education given children in the Eighteenth Century when children were usually brought up as hothouse plants, and forced intellectually under harsh discipline. The work outraged the Church by removing the training of the child from the hands of the clergy, and by preaching deism. The Archbishop of Paris condemned the book, and wrote a refutation. It was also condemned by the Sorbonne, and the Parlement of Paris, and Rousseau became a hunted fugitive.

Rousseau continued his earlier practice of frequently changing his place of residence. This was due to his innate restlessness, to his desire to be alone, and to his attempts to escape the public authorities. He spent some time in England as a guest of a Hume who found him difficult, and with whom Rousseau quarrelled. He was like a man, declared Hume, who has his skin off! In 1782, after his death, Rousseau's *Confessions* were published. Here he says, near the beginning, "I am not made like any other man in the world. If I am not better, at least, I am different." The work is a remarkably frank portrait with a penetrating analysis of his character though it contains some needless details particularly about his childhood and youth.

This is combined with charming descriptions of nature, and the work is spiced with eroticism. His *Reveries of a Solitary Stroller* continue the *Confessions*; its chief emphasis is on the inspiring and consoling effects of wild nature on the spirit of man. The *Confessions* and the *Reveries*, though published after Rousseau's death, caused a sensation. He had started a current of subjective literature which was continued by Goethe in Germany, Chateaubriand in France, and Wordsworth and Byron in England. The story is told that one day the citizens of Königsberg in Prussia noticed that Kant was not taking his daily walk, and it was discovered later that he had been reading Rousseau's *Confessions*! Horace Walpole declared that the *Confessions* was the most disgusting book he had ever read.

In his later years, Rousseau became increasingly suspicious even of those who tried to befriend him, and he imagined plots to ruin or betray him. These delusions of persecution made his last years miserable.

Rousseau's influence was enormous. He spread a new respect for the common man, a love of common things, a sense of pity, and the feeling that much in the life of the time was artificial. He made tears the fashion, and he became the wellspring of modern humanitarianism. "Your writings," Boswell told Rousseau, "have melted my heart, elevated my soul, and kindled my imagination." As a result of his teachings, Arthur Young said in 1787 that the French nobles now preferred to live in their country seats, and that their wives were ashamed of not suckling their babies.

Rousseau had an enormous influence on the people whose convictions, needs, aspirations, hatreds, and prejudices he had so perfectly expressed. Men sick with oppression, poverty, and despair hailed Rousseau, the denouncer of kings, the scorner of nobles, and the advocate of the lowly. More than any other Philosophe, Rousseau gave men faith in their power to redress the wrongs of ages. Rousseau was denounced by Burke and Joseph de Maistre, as he has been denounced by many others since. But he was praised by the Jacobins of the French Revolution, and hailed by the German and English Romantics. Certainly none of the Philosophes, except perhaps Voltaire, had a greater influence, and Rousseau's influence turned the course of many fields of thought. Ethical, educational, political, religious, artistic, literary, and musical thought were never the same again.

CONCLUSION

The Philosophes of the Enlightenment in France, as we have seen, either founded or advanced all the social sciences. Also many of the reforms they projected were extremely practical, and a large number of them were later enacted into law or accepted by the mass of men. The whole idea of the Philosophes as being doctrinaire theorists without relation to actual conditions can no longer be held.

"The Philosophes," says one historian, "taught that by reason man may be the master of things, that he can build a society in which all men enjoy freedom and happiness, that he can deliberately create the society he has imagined. They directed their most powerful views against the traditional and clerical view that our lives are in His hands, that man is a creature fallen and perverse who cannot be saved from self-destruction except through the gift of grace, and must bow his individual reason before the sublime authority of Church and state."

The influence of the Philosophes on the coming of the French Revolution and on its course of action began to be discussed by Burke as early as 1791, and the discussion has gone on ever since. In general, writers of a Conservative turn of mind have tended to blame the French Revolution on the spread of the Liberal and Radical ideas of the Philosophes. On the other hand, critics of a Liberal or Radical point of view have considered the French Revolution as the result of abuses in the Old Regime. On the side of the Liberal Radical thinkers has been the fact that in the *Cahiers*, lists of grievances prepared for the consideration of the Estates General before 1789, there is little mention of the Philosophes.

Actually, the French Revolution seems to have begun in France rather than in Spain or Sicily or elsewhere because conditions were getting better in France during the Eighteenth Century, at least for the more well-to-do classes, but they were not getting better fast enough. So the coming of the French Revolution seems to have been the result of both abuses and programs of reform as proposed by the Philosophes.

As one modern historian has said, "Surely if the Old Regime had been threatened only by ideas it would have run no risk. Ideas needed a fulcrum, the people's misery and unrest, in order to be effective. But these practical causes would not have sufficed to bring about the Revolution as rapidly as it came. It was ideas that demonstrated and systematized the consequences of unrest and initiated the movement for the calling of the Estates General."

After the Revolution began, its political, educational, and religious policies clearly show the influence of the Philosophes. The *Constitution of 1791* shows the influence of Montesquieu, and the *Constitution of 1793* bears the marks of the theories of Rousseau. The worship of Reason was Voltairian, and the worship of the Supreme Being of the Age of the Convention shows the influence of Rousseau. So the political, religious, social, and educational acts of the Revolution clearly reflect the influence of the Philosophes, and their influence is very marked in the course of events of the Nineteenth and Twentieth Centuries.

BIBLIOGRAPHY

Some anthologies of writings by the Philosophes

C. Brinton, ed. *The Age of Reason reader* (New York, 1956), the fullest collection, divides the material by subjects rather than by writers; N. Torrey, ed. *The Philosophes* (New York, 1960); F. E. Manuel, ed. *The Enlightenment* (New York, 1965); I. Berlin, ed. *The Age of Enlightenment* (New York, 1951); and L. L. Snyder, ed. *The Age of Reason* (New York, 1955).

General Works

D. C. Cabeen, ed. *Critical bibliography of French literature* Vol. IV *The Eighteenth Century* (Syracuse, 1951); P. Amann, ed. *The Eighteenth Century Revolution* (Boston, 1963); J. L. Talmon, *Origins of totalitarian democracy* (New York, 1960); K. Martin, *French liberal thought in the 18th century* (2nd ed. London, 1962), the best general introduction; G. R. Havens, *The age of ideas* (New York, 1955), an excellent popularization by a leading authority; C. Becker, *The heavenly city of the 18th century philosophers* (New Haven, 1932), a brilliant interpretation that, however, has been frequently challenged, cf. R. O. Rockwood, ed. *Becker's heavenly city revisited* (Ithaca, 1958); P. Smith, *History of modern culture*, Vol. II (New York 1934); J. H. Randall, *The career of philosophy* (2 vols., New York, 1962); J. H. Randall, *Making of the modern mind* (2nd ed. Boston, 1940), very condensed but a masterpiece; C. Brinton, *Ideas and men* (2nd ed. New York, 1963), an excellent survey by a leading authority; F. J. C. Hearnshaw, ed. *The social and political ideas of some*

* This is a summary bibliography of works easily available.

154

great French thinkers of the Age of Reason (London, 1930); R. Anchor, *The Enlightenment tradition* (New York, 1967); P. Gay, *Age of Enlightenment* (New York, 1966), a good popularization; and by the same author, *The Enlightenment, an interpretation,* Vol. I (New York, 1966), a masterpiece; both works of Gay treat the Enlightenment all over Europe; P. Gay, *The party of humanity* (New York, 1964), a collection of admirable interpretative essays; E. Faguet, *Etudes littéraires, le 18ᵉ siècle* (n.d. Paris); C. Sainte-Beuve, *Portraits of the 18th century* (2 vols., New York, 1905); J. Bédier and P. Hazard, *Histoire de la littérature française* (New ed. 2 vols., Paris, 1950); L. I. Bredvold, *Brave new world of the Enlightenment* (Ann Arbor, 1961), very critical of the Philosophes; J. B. Bury, *History of the freedom of thought* (2nd ed. Oxford, 1952), brief but penetrating; E. Cassirer, *Philosophy of the Enlightenment* (Princeton, 1951), considered by many historians as the best book on the Enlightenment, hard to read; H. Dieckman, "An interpretation of the 18th century" in *Modern language quarterly,* 1954, a fine review of Cassirer's book; A. Cobban, *In search of humanity, role of the Enlightenment in modern history* (London, 1960), a good introduction; J. J. Crocker, *An age of crisis, man and the world in 18th century French thought* (Baltimore, 1959); and by the same author, *Nature and culture, ethical thought in the French Enlightenment* (Baltimore, 1963); both are profound studies; A. L. Guérard, *Life and death of an ideal* (New York, 1928); B. Fay, *The Revolutionary Spirit in France and America* (New York, 1927); A. R. Hall, *The scientific revolution, 1500-1800* (New York, 1954); P. Hazard, *European thought in the 18th century* (London, 1954), very readable; M. Kraus, "America and the Utopian ideals in the 18th century" in *Mississippi Valley historical review,* 1936; F. A. Lange, *History of materialism* (New York, 1950); W. E. H. Lecky, *History of the rise and influence of rationalism in Europe* (rev. ed. New York, 1914); J. M. Robertson, *Short history of free thought* (2nd ed. London, 1906); H. J. Laski, *Rise of Euro-*

pean Liberalism (London, 1947); G. de Ruggiero, *History of European Liberalism* (Oxford, 1927); A. O. Lovejoy, *The great chain of being* (Cambridge, Mass., 1936); D. Mornet, *Les origines intellectuelles de la Révolution française* (Paris, 1933), an important work; and by the same author, *French thought in the 18th Century* (New York, 1929), slight; R. B. Mowat, *The age of reason* (London, 1934); L. Réau, *L'Europe française au siècle des lumières* (Paris, 1938); W. A. Dunning, *Political thought from Luther to Montesquieu* (New York, 1916); and by the same author, *Political thought from Rousseau to Spenser* (New York, 1920); G. Sabine, *History of political theory* (3rd. ed. New York, 1961), a masterpiece; H. Sée, *L'Evolution de la pensée politique en France au 18ᵉ siècle*, (Paris, 1925); and by the same author, *Les idées politiques en France au 18ᵉ siècle* (Paris, 1920); J. S. Spink, *French free thought from Gassendi to Voltaire* (London, 1960); H. Vyverberg, *Historical pessimism in the French Enlightenment* (Cambridge, Mass., 1958); A. Wolf, *History of science, technology and philosophy—18th Century* (2nd ed. London, 1952); F. E. Manuel, *The 18th century confronts the Gods*, (Cambridge, Mass., 1959); R. R. Palmer, *Catholics and unbelievers in 18th century France* (Princeton, 1939); E. G. Barber, *The bourgeoisie in 18th century France* (Princeton, 1955); A. Goodwin, ed. *European nobility in the 18th century* (London, 1953); F. L. Baumer, *Religion and the rise of skepticism* (New York, 1960); L. Cahen, *Les querrelles religieuses et parlementaires sous Louis XV* (Paris, 1913); J. W. Gough, *The social contract* (2nd ed. Oxford, 1957); and W. F. Church, ed. *The influence of the Enlightenment on the French Revolution* (Boston, 1964), a very useful selection of texts from Burke to the present.

The Precursors of the Philosophes

E. Bréhier, *History of philosophy—17th century* (Chicago, 1967), a thorough introduction; E. A. Burtt, *The metaphysical foundations of modern physical science* (2nd ed. London, 1959); H. Butterfield, *Origins of modern science, 1300-1800* (2nd ed. London, 1958); A. R. Hall, *The scientific revolution, 1500-1800* (New York, 1954); L. Rothkrug, *Opposition to Louis XIV, political and social origins of the French Enlightenment* (Princeton, 1965); M. Dréano, *La renommée de Montaigne en France au 18ᵉ siècle* (Paris, 1952); P. Villey-Desmerets, *L'influence de Montaigne sur les idées pédagogiques de Locke et de Rousseau* (Paris, 1911); J. H. Anderson, *Bacon* (Los Angeles, 1962); C. D. Bowen, *Bacon, the temper of the man* (Boston, 1963); P. Vernière, *Spinoza et la pensée française avant la Révolution* (2 vols., Paris, 1954); S. Hampshire, *Spinoza* (London, 1951); H. F. Hallett, *Spinoza* (London, 1957); J. Dunner, *Spinoza and Western democracy* (New York, 1955); W. H. Barber, *Leibniz in France* (Oxford, 1955); R. W. Meyer, *Leibniz and the 17th century revolution* (Cambridge, 1952); R. L. Saw, *Leibniz* (London, 1951); J. Bowle, *Hobbes and his critics* (London, 1951); R. S. Peters, *Hobbes* (London, 1956); T. E. Jessop, *Hobbes* (London, 1960); K. C. Brown, ed. *Hobbes, studies* (Cambridge, Mass., 1965); P. Brunet, *L'introduction des théories de Newton en France au 18ᵉ siècle*, (Paris, 1931); History of science society, ed. *Newton, a bicentenary evaluation* (Baltimore, 1928); E. N. Andrade, *Newton* (London, 1954); R. H. Hurlbutt, *Hume, Newton and the design argument* (Lincoln, 1965); H. Sootin, *Newton* (New York, 1955); L. T. More, *Newton* (new ed. New York, 1962); R. I. Aaron, *Locke,* (2nd ed. Oxford, 1955); M. W. Cranston, *Locke, a biography* (London, 1957); G. D. Bonno, *Les relations intellectuelles de Locke avec la France* (Berkeley, 1955), on French influences on Locke; A. G. A. Balz, *Descartes and the modern mind* (New Haven, 1952); A. Koyré, *Descartes after three hundred years* (Buffalo, 1951); H. T. Barnwell, *Les idées morales et critiques de Saint-Évremond* (Paris, 1957); J. R. Carré, *La philosophie de Fontenelle* (Paris, 1932); L. M. Marsak, "Fontenelle, the idea of science in the French Enlightenment" in *Transac-*

158   THE ENLIGHTENMENT IN FRANCE

tions of the American Philosophical Society 1959; K. D. Little, *Fénelon* (New York, 1951); J. L. Gore, *L'itinéraire de Fénelon, humanisme et spiritualité* (Paris, 1957); L. Cogret, *Crépuscule des mystiques, le conflit Fénelon-Bossuet* (Tournai, 1958); E. Carcassonne, *Fénelon, l'homme et l'oeuvre* (Paris, 1946); R. H. Popkin, *History of skepticism from Erasmus to Descartes* (New ed. New York, 1964); R. H. Popkin, ed. *Bayle's historical and critical dictionary, selections* (Indianapolis, 1965); E. A. Beller and M. P. Lee, eds. *Selections from Bayle's dictionary* (Princeton, 1952); H. Robinson, *Bayle the skeptic* (New York, 1931); E. Labrousse, *Bayle* (12 vols., The Hague, 1963-4); P. Bilon and R. H. Popkin, ed. *Bayle, etudes et documents* (Amsterdam, 1959); W. Rex, *Essays on Bayle* (The Hague, 1965); K. C. Sandberg, *At the crossroads of faith and reason, Bayle* (Tucson, 1966), the last four works have modified older ideas about Bayle; H. T. Mason, *Bayle and Voltaire* (London, 1963); and L. P. Courtines, *Bayle's relations with England* (New York, 1938).

Salons

R. Picard, *Les salons littéraires et la société française, 1610-1789* (New York, 1943); and M. Glotz and M. Maire, *Les salons au 18ᵉ siècle* (Paris, 1944).

Censorship and the book trade

J. P. Belin, *Le commerce des livres prohibés à Paris, 1750-1789* (Paris, 1913); L. Cohen, "La librairie parisienne et la diffusion des idées françaises à la fin du 18ᵉ siècle" in *Revue de synthèse historique*, 1939; I. Wade, *The clandestine organization of philosphic ideas in France, 1700-1750* (Princeton, 1938); and D. Mornet, "Les enseignements des bibliothèques privées, 1750-1780" in *Revue d'histoire littéraire de la France, 1910*.

Montesquieu

D. C. Cabeen, ed. *Montesquieu, a bibliography* (New York, 1947); the two best books on Montesquieu are J. Dedieu, *Montesquieu, l'homme et l'oeuvre* (Paris, 1943) and R. Shackleton, *Montesquieu, a critical biography* (Oxford, 1961), and they supplement each other; cf. also, R. Aron, *Main currents in sociological thought* Vol. I (New York, 1965); G. Bonno, *La constitution britannique devant l'opinion française de Montesquieu à Bonaparte* (Paris, 1932); E. Carcassonne, *Montesquieu et le problème de la constitution française au 18e siècle* (Paris, 1927); F. T. Fletcher, *Montesquieu and English politics, 1750-1800* (London, 1939); and L. L. Levin, *Political doctrine of Montesquieu's 'Esprit des lois'* (New York, 1936).

Voltaire

R. B. Redman, ed. *Portable Voltaire* (New York, 1949); N. L. Torrey, ed. *Voltaire and the Enlightenment* (New York, 1931); J. Orieux, *Voltaire* (Paris, 1966), the best biography; G. Lanson, *Voltaire* (New York, 1966), the best short life; R. Naves, *Voltaire, l'homme et l'oeuvre* (Paris, 1942); N. L. Torrey, *Spirit of Voltaire* (New York, 1938); R. Pomeau, *La religion de Voltaire* (Mizet, 1956); N. L. Torrey, *Voltaire and the English deists* (New Haven, 1930); D. D. Bren, *The Calas affair* (Princeton, 1960); J. H. Brumfitt, *Voltaire, historian* (Oxford, 1958); M. Dommanget, *Le curé Meslier* (Paris, 1965); P. Gay, ed. *Voltaire's philosophic dictionary* (New York, 1962); P. Gay, *Voltaire's politics* (Princeton, 1959); M. S. Libby, *The attitude of Voltaire to magic and the sciences* (London, 1935); M. T. Maestro, *Voltaire and Beccaria as reformers of criminal law* (New York, 1942); H. T. Mason, *Bayle and Voltaire* (Oxford, 1963); and I. Wade, *Voltaire and Mme de Châtelet* (Princeton, 1941).

160 THE ENLIGHTENMENT IN FRANCE

Diderot

L. G. Crocker, ed. *Diderot, selected writings* (New York, 1966);
L. G. Crocker, *Diderot* (New York, 1966), the best biography; H.
Gillot, *Diderot* (Paris, 1937); H. Lefebre, *Diderot* (Paris, 1941);
D. Mornet, *Diderot* (Paris, 1941); A. M. Wilson, *Diderot, the test-
ing years, 1713-1759* (Oxford, 1957), a masterpiece; O. E. Fellows
and N. T. Torrey, eds. *Diderot Studies* (7 vols., Syracuse, 1950); J.
Oestreicher, *La pensée politique et économique de Diderot* (Vincennes, 1936); J. Lough, ed. *Encyclopédie, selected articles* (Cam-
bridge, 1954); S. Gendzier, ed. *The Encyclopedia, selections* (New
York, 1966); J. Proust, *L'Encyclopédie* (Paris, 1965), best study of
the *Encyclopedia;* J. Le Gras, *Diderot et l'Encyclopédie* (Amiens,
1929); L. Thorndike, "L'Encyclopédie and the history of science" in
Isis, 1924; D. H. Gordon and N. L. Torrey, *The censoring of Diderot's
Encyclopédie* (New York, 1947); R. Hubert, *Les sciences sociales
dans l'Encyclopédie* (Paris, 1923), an important study; J. E. Baker,
Diderot's treatment of the Christian religion (New York, 1941);
R. L. Cru, *Diderot as a disciple of English thought* (New York,
1913); and J. Seznec, *Diderot et l'antiquité* (Oxford, 1957).

The Physiocrats

C. Gide and C. Rist, *History of economic doctrines* (2nd English ed.
Boston, 1948); H. Higgs, *The Physiocrats* (London, 1897), only
longer treatment in English; G. Weulersse, *Les Physiocrats* (Paris,
1931), best general discussion; and three detailed works by the same
author, *Le mouvement physiocratique, 1756-1770* (2 vols., Paris,
1916); *La physiocratie sous Turgot et Necker, 1774-1781* (Paris,
1950), and *La physiocratie à la fin du règne de Louis XV* (Paris,
1959).

Abbé de Saint-Pierre

M. L. Perkins, *The moral and political philosophy at the Abbé de Saint-Pierre* (Geneva, 1959).

La Mettrie

R. Boissier, *La Mettrie* (Paris, 1931); and A. Vartanian, *La Mettrie's 'Homme machine'* (Princeton, 1960).

Holbach

P. Naville, *Holbach* (Paris, 1943); and W. H. Wickwar, *Holbach* (New York, 1935).

Helvétius

I. L. Horowitz, *Helvétius* (New York, 1954); A. Keim, *Helvétius* (Paris, 1907); D. W. Smith, *Helvétius* (Oxford, 1965); and I. Cumming, *Helvétius, his life and place in the history of educational thought* (London, 1955).

Condillac

Z. Schaupp, *The naturalism of Condillac* (Lincoln, 1926).

Condorcet

J. B. Bury, *Idea of progress* (New ed. New York, 1955); J. Devaille, *Essai sur l'histoire de l'idée de progrès jusqu'à la fin du 18ᵉ siècle* (Paris, 1910); C. Frankel, *The faith of reason, the idea of progress in the French Enlightenment* (New York, 1948); R. V. Sampson, *Progress in the Age of Reason* (London, 1956); F. J. Teggart, ed. *The idea of progress* (Berkeley, 1925); L. Cahen, *Condorcet et la Révolution française* (Paris, 1904); and J. S. Shapiro, *Condorcet and the rise of Liberalism* (New York, 1963), a thorough study.

Mably and Morelly

A. Gray, *The Socialist tradition* (New York, 1946); A. Lichtenberger, *Le Socialisme français au 18ᵉ siècle* (Paris, 1895).

Rousseau

There is an admirable bibliographical article on Rousseau in P. Gay, *The party of humanity* (New York, 1964); J. Guéhenno, *Rousseau* (2 vols., New York, 1966), now the best biography; F. C. Green, *Rousseau* (Cambridge, 1955); C. W. Hendel, *Rousseau, moralist* (2 vols., Indianapolis, 1962), a fundamental study; E. Cassirer, *The question of Rousseau* (Bloomington, 1963), very penetrating study; E. H. Wright, *The meaning of Rousseau* (Oxford, 1929); I. Babbitt, *Rousseau and Romanticism* (Boston, 1919), typical of an extensive literature hostile to Rousseau; two works by R. Derathé, *Le rationalisme de Rousseau* (Paris, 1948); and by the same author, *Rousseau et la science politique de son temps* (Paris, 1950), both are admirable; M. Einaudi, *The early Rousseau* (Ithaca, 1967); and H. N. Fairchild, *The noble savage* (New York, 1928).

INDEX